ARE YOU LIST

GW00598861

It's good to have someone to talk to when you have a lot on your mind, and Jay has always been pretty close to his elder sister, Karen. The only trouble is, she's dead now, killed in a motor accident before he had a chance to tell her about the really important things that have been happening to him recently. Still, he needs to get it off his chest, and when he visits her grave, who knows, she *might* be listening.

He wants to tell her about sixth-form college, and how much he'd love to be free of it if he had the courage. But how can he disappoint their mum, struggling to bring up a family without a husband to help, and made extra bitter by the knowledge that dad's soon getting married again? That's another thing Jay's been meaning to talk to Karen about – but most of all, he longs to tell her about Hannah.

Jay never thought he'd fall hopelessly for a girl, but Hannah really knocked him out. The good part was, she seemed to like him, and because nobody else mattered to him now he found the guts to stand up to the crowd he usually hung around with. He stopped thinking he had to buy dope, or listen to music he hated, or attack poor Cookie, who never had any luck with girls, just so he could fit in with the rest. The bad part was – well, that came a bit later. But whether she's listening or not, Jay feels better for talking to Karen.

Funny and touching by turns, *Are You Listening, Karen?* is a highly readable, intensely convincing story of a teenage boy straining to make sense of himself and his world. David Day doesn't pull any punches, doesn't provide an easy up-beat ending – with skill and conviction, he just tells it like it is.

David Day wrote this book at the age of 17. He studied Social Psychology at Loughborough University. His many interests include music, dogs and football.

David Day

Are You Listening, Karen?

Puffin Books

Puffin Books, Penguin Books Ltd, Harmondsworth, Middlesex, England
Viking Penguin Inc., 40 West 23rd Street, New York, New York 10010, U.S.A.
Penguin Books Australia Ltd, Ringwood, Victoria, Australia
Penguin Books Canada Limited, 2801 John Street, Markham, Ontario,
Canada L3R 1B4
Penguin Books (N.Z.) Ltd, 182–190 Wairau Road, Auckland 10, New Zealand

First published by André Deutsch Ltd 1983
Published in Puffin Books 1985
Reprinted 1987

Copyright © David Day, 1983
All rights reserved

Printed and bound in Great Britain by
Cox & Wyman Ltd, Reading
Typeset in Baskerville

Except in the United States of America,
this book is sold subject to the condition·
that it shall not, by way of trade or otherwise,
be lent, re-sold, hired out, or otherwise circulated
without the publisher's prior consent in any form of
binding or cover other than that in which it is
published and without a similar condition
including this condition being imposed
on the subsequent purchaser

ONE

It's drizzling out here, Karen. I expect it's cold and all but I can't feel it because I've been doing the old jogging. Yes, I still do it, every day now; round the block three times without fail. Another routine to go through, that's all. Gets me through the day, so I can't complain.

Anyway I thought I'd pop in and see how you're getting along. I haven't brought you any flowers to liven the place up, I'm afraid. It really is the stereotyped view of a graveyard; cold, dark and quiet. Not scary though, I'm not scared of the place, Karen. By the way, you're rested between an old dear who passed away in 1952 aged eighty-three and a middle-aged gentleman by the name of George Campton. I expect you're already acquainted.

Well, I'm here because I've wanted to talk to you for some time and I didn't get a proper chance to see you alone that Friday. You weren't half the centre of attention, Karen; everyone was there. Aunts, uncles, cousins, nieces and unknown relations from places like Fife. Hell, I didn't know we had so many relations, we never got Christmas presents from them, did we? It was quite funny in a way because of all the people there that Friday, it was these jokers that I'd never seen in my life who were bawling their eyes out for you and shouting their mouths off about what a tragedy it was. And there at the front of the church were Mum and Dad sitting silently, with cold, grey faces and eyes glazed. So dignified, Karen, it was incredible.

You'll be glad to know that the vicar who took the service was the young, trendy one that you fancied. He said loads of nice things about you as well. He made it sound really good.

1

'Karen Border was a kind and sweet child of the Lord who spread love wherever she went.' Yeah, I think he may have just slightly overdone it.

It was during the boring bits that I kept thinking about what had happened to me in my last six months or so. I know it sounds selfish, but it isn't really. You see, you and Ed were the only possible people that I could ever have talked to properly and I can hardly tell a six-year-old about my teenage problems, can I? Now I'm the first to admit that we didn't talk much about deep things and all that, but if there was anybody I was close to, it was you.

OK, I expect you're wondering what I'm rambling on about, but you see, if your glorious boyfriend, Richard D. Ives, hadn't driven you into a tree, I would have told you everything I've kept inside of me.

In my naivete, I figured you'd survive long enough for Christmas. Hell, it was only a week until the Christmas holidays. Ed was all looking forward to giving you his present that he was so proud of. But it never happened and now no one will ever know how I feel.

Do you realise, Karen, how much things have changed since that first Monday in September last year? I remember it clearly, even now. The day that crops up every year, the first time in weeks that I had to drag myself out of bed before mid-day. A morning of hazy sunshine, a rushed breakfast of cornflakes (which Mum forced down me because she reckoned it was bad for me not to have any breakfast), a race to catch the 526 bus which left the corner at 8.06. Yes, you've guessed it, the day every kid rings in his calendar, the first day of the new school year.

It was slightly different and all, last year. I'd been used to getting up with you around, but now you'd hopped off to Durham University to 'further your education', and gone off early to find somewhere to live or something, so it was just Ed and me. Yes, I had the burden that you'd previously taken on, of putting up with his wild games and antics. Not the sort of responsibility I enjoyed early in the morning.

What's more, it was a new school for me (wow, what

excitement). Cartland Sixth Form College; a place for the keen, the intelligent, the scholarly – and I went as well. A school that I knew would be the same drag as all the other schools had been. But let's face it, Karen, I had only myself to blame for going there. I had fantasies of bursting free the day I left the old fifth form, never to return to an 'educational institution' again. But I was back. Sure, it was officially a different school, but deep down I knew it would be just the same as the old one.

So Cartland it was, though I'd probably not have got in without the help of Mum. I'm not sure what I was dreading most, the hours of boring work ahead or the bloody uniform. How I'd sworn never to go to Cartland because of the uniform. Well, who wants to wear green, Karen? I remember you cursing the world when you first put your uniform on. 'They'll all laugh at me,' you cried. Typical overreaction on your part. Only when you realised that every other 6th former looked as much of a pratt as you, did you cool down.

It being a sixth form college and all, I expected Cartland to be different. But somehow as I walked through the wooden, crumbling gates I realised I'd seen this all before. Red, rustic buildings, thirty or forty years old; smallish, echoing corridors along the rectangular, symmetrical structure. The plasticky effect of the whole – whitewashed walls, polished floors and little displays showing off what the school had achieved. You know what I mean, the cups and plaques telling us all that Cartland's sixth form cricketers were champions for two years in a row. And the smell, Karen, surely you haven't forgotten that? Carl described it as a cross between the cleaning lotion used by the caretakers and the left-overs from the school dinners. Yeah, walking through that school had about the same inspirational value as watching cement set.

I always went to school with Justin. What fond memories you must hold of him. 'Shallow and immature' was your most common description of my friend. See how I can recall all those things you said about us! You knew long before me that I went round with morons, but I used to laugh at you. Justin had been my mate since junior school. It was funny that we'd kept together right up to Cartland. Not that we were close, him being so with-it. Remember, Karen, he had hair like Olivia Newton-John, a great mane of blond locks.

The thing about him was that in the mornings he was always so lively, real full of it, he was. He'd get up at 5.30 and have a shower and do a paper round, so he'd be properly awake by the time school came around, in contrast to me, who never runs on full cylinders until about 11.30. Boy, was I lousy in the mornings and I mean lousy. That morning in September had been even more of a hassle because Ed had one of his tantrums; he'd told Mum that he didn't want to go to school any more because he hadn't finished doing his Rubic cube. And guess who had to go into his room and sort the pest out, only to get booted in the balls when I nicked his cube.

'Cheer up, Jay,' Justin said breezily as we walked toward the new school. 'Think of what we've got to look forward to in the next two years.'

He was sarky, was Justin. Like me!

'Like what?' I moaned.

'A chance to nourish your undoubted intellectual ability.'

'Oh super,' I said in my posh voice.

'To meet new people.'

'Lovely.'

'A new experience, a challenge,' he continued excitedly, with a smile on his face resembling that of a Cheshire cat. It really was uncanny, that smile he had.

'Oh wrap up, Justin,' I blew out. 'I'm knackered.'

I really did have the 'get up at 7.30' blues, I wasn't in the land of the living. I yawned loudly as we approached the front gates and the newly painted sign which said boldly in black paint 'CARTLAND SIXTH FORM COLLEGE'. I looked up at the sign briefly, sighed and went in. It was a slightly nervous moment, where you're not sure what's going to happen next. You must have felt like that, Karen. We passed muddles of people talking together in groups;

4

some I recognised from Jenny High, but they looked different people in the new uniform. Other people were totally new to me. I felt almost insecure because of this mysterious element of people. I've always felt worried about meeting new friends. That's one of the things that I'm funny about. Not one of your major problems, was it?

'Hey look, Jay,' Justin pointed to two birds in the corner of the playground, diagonally opposite us. I hardly recognised them at first. 'It's Sylvia and Kay.'

He'd always had his eyes on Sylvia, without much luck, but it wasn't for the lack of trying.

'Yeah, I see them.'

'So let's have a word.'

'Oh don't bother . . .' I started; but he pulled me over by the sleeve of my coat so I hadn't much choice but to follow him. 'It's too early to be friendly,' I drawled hopelessly. He wasn't listening anyway.

'Hey, girls,' he called in his macho, chatting-up-birds voice.

'Hi-ya,' Sylvia, the red-head, answered him, whilst simultaneously chewing her gum. She was attractive, sure, but a bit abrasive if you know what I mean. A slight pain in the ass if there is such a thing. She was a bit like that Terry girl you went round with, the one you tried to avoid. I preferred the other one, but she didn't say much.

'You have a good holiday?' said Justin.

'Yeah, great. I went to Southern France; it was really nice, dead sunny,' answered Sylvia.

'Ah, that's nice.'

'You look brown,' I added.

'Yeah, guess I am,' she said, chewing unceasingly. 'But I tend to go bright red and peel.'

'Do you?' I replied, trying to sound interested. I felt I had to say something to keep in the conversation.

'Ah-ha.'

'I went on holiday, too,' said Justin.

'Good, where d'you go?'

He paused for once and went slightly red.

'Manchester,' he murmured.

'You what?'

'Manchester,' he said louder.

I laughed, it was about the funniest thing that had happened that day. The girls looked at each other as if to laugh but out of politeness they kept quiet.

'That's OK,' said Sylvia. I sniggered. 'I'm sure there are things to do in Manchester.'

'Like what?' I sneered.

'I went to the International Home Festival.'

'I bet you fainted with the thrill.'

'Look mate,' he said (he always said mate when he got annoyed), 'you're getting up my nose.'

I think the birds had had enough of our petty argument and they filtered away. Justin looked on, stunned that his true loves were gone. Then he turned toward me, Olivia Newton-John hairstyle and all. He glared me a mean glare. Yes, I'm sure you would put the blame on me in that argument, Karen. That 'immaturity' shining through. I can see you shaking your head now. Don't overreact, sister, I was only kidding around.

'Now they've gone. Cheers Jay,' Justin moaned. 'I'll do the same for you sometime.'

'Sure,' I smiled. Poor Justin.

As we spoke, loads of our mates approached, the old gang from Jenny High. Marshall, Cookie and Carl had all made it to the Sixth Form. A true miracle that most of us had actually come back for more, Cartland didn't know what it had let itself in for by allowing our group in. We had the potential to turn that place from a school to a mental institution. Not that there's a lot of difference.

I never could work out how I always ended up with this mob, not that anyone was super-naughty, but simply we were a bunch of dossers, the rebels. You know the scene, Karen. The way we competed and pushed each other about to get noticed. The fighting for popularity. I hardly realised what I was a part of.

Never mind, I was happy to see the lads.

'Hey, you're all here, amazing.'

'Not as amazing as you being here. Thought you'd be on the dole queue,' said Carl, typically the first to speak.

'The only one I thought'd be here is Cookie,' said Marshall, the handsome brute of our group.

Cookie shrugged his shoulders.

'I nearly didn't come here.'

'Look, Cookie, you can't go to Oxbridge yet. Not even you. Qualifications first, Cookie.'

By the way, Karen, his real name was Martin Woodley not Cookie and don't ask me how he got the nickname. Cookie was always the unfortunate kid, the one I felt sorriest for. The one you'd have felt for. I don't know why he got teased so much; possibly because he worked hard or maybe his appearance; short and stocky with thick metal-rimmed glasses which built up an image as a boff. Stupid really, some kids I know with specs can't spell their name.

He always laughed insults off, did Cookie. Pretended they didn't matter. Oh Karen, it must have eaten him up.

'Hey, lads,' I said, changing the subject, 'did you see Justin chatting up those birds?'

'Who?' said Marshall, always eager to know about anything connected with birds.

'Sylvia Tremlett.'

'Ah, slag,' he said, combing his hair back with one of the set of combs which he replaced every week. I can see it now, Karen. He hardly ever had a single hair out of place, not a single one. Very depressing. And while I'm discussing Marshall I might as well discuss his clothing habits. He'd come to school with his shirt buttons undone and ponging of the sort of aftershave you buy at Fenwicks.

'What did he say then?' said Carl.

'It was funny, I'm telling you. He was discussing his holiday. "I had a great time," he said. "Where d'you go?" she said, "Manchester," he said.'

Laughs all round, except Justin.

'It's better than saying nothing, like you.'

'I don't fancy her anyway.'

'What, Sylvia?' he gasped in disbelief. 'How can you say that?'

'Quite easily.'

'She's got to be at least a 6.2 on the Richter Scale.'

'6.2, no way; more like a 5.3, 5.4.'

No, Karen, this isn't secret code, but a way of marking you females on a scale of 1 to 10. Surely you've passed kids in the corridor and they've said a number out of the blue. When we say it like that, birds don't know what's going on at all. Actually, if you think about it, the Richter Scale could be real upsetting to some birds, but no one thinks about it, do they? I expect you lot give boys a mark and all; don't tell me mine. I don't want to hear it.

At 8.50 sharp we were ushered into the large hall in the main school building. We all knew what this meant as we entered, the famous 'Headmaster's opening speech'. The lines of seats were laid out for us and having sat down we only had to wait for Mr Gore. Ah, Mr Gore, very purposeful and intent, an ageing man who must have done this thirty times before. He strutted to the front and as he did so he looked at the people in the hall, smiling like a phoney as he went. The only reason you liked him was because he called you 'Karen'. He only called pretty birds by their first names. What a pain.

Carl whispered in my ear as he reached the front of the room ready to speak to his waiting audience. 'He's going to tell us how pleased he is to have us at his school.'

'Good morning,' said old Gore as he started his speech. We all slumped ourselves into comfortable sleeping positions. 'Welcome to our College, and that is a welcome on behalf of not only myself but the entire staff who hope to make your stay a profitable one.'

It makes you wonder whether every headmaster in the country is programmed to say those exact words on opening day. It's so drab, Karen. Do you think they share a handbook? Chapter 1 must be 'How to speak to the new students'. Temporarily, I forgot that this was the Sixth

Form where everyone was mature and sensible, because I half expected someone to fart. Silly me.

It's almost ironic, me laughing at the bloke as I did then, because what he said next was to become true.

'This will, for all of you, be the most important year of your life.'

Very astute and wise, huh? (Sorry! I'm being sarcastic again.) But, coincidentally, he was right this time. It's all changed so much since that day. I look back on those days (really so recent) with a kind of nostalgia. Oh yes, the days when my biggest problems were keeping up with homework, and not being late for football practice. So simple, Karen, so simple.

And in these nostalgic moments I wonder what might have happened if I hadn't have gone to Cartland. After all, I only just got into the place. It was all due to Mum, she wanted the best for us kids and I could tell she was dying for me to follow in your footsteps through the Sixth Form. You know, Karen, you've really got a lot to answer for. You being so successful, Mum wants me to at least match it. 'If you worked as hard as Karen, you could succeed as well.' That was the exact word, 'succeed'.

The trouble always came on the day that we brought back our reports and she could compare them. Jason Border, Form 5B, 'has definite ability but lacks concentration and appears uninterested at times'. Isn't that a terrific way of saying I was bone idle, but it didn't fool Mum.

But I had got in to Cartland, after a few discussions with the staff, and Mum had something to boast about to the neighbours.

'So how's your Jason doing at school?'

'Oh very well, thank you. He's taking two A levels.'

'How wonderful. Our Jean is doing three.'

How wonderful.

TWO

Perhaps I started feeling different from that Sunday when
we met Jill. It broke the routine. After all, Sundays were
always specifically Dad day. Ed and me picked up at 9.00
and back by 7.30 or there was trouble from Mum. Mornings
were usually golf, me caddying for Dad and Ed left behind
with Alex's wife. You never did meet Alex, did you? He was
one of Dad's buddies at work, a true Scot he was, 'Och aye,
the noo'. There were times when I could have used an
interpreter. On top of that he threw his money about like a
Jock. On Sunday, his caddie was off ill so I did his clubs as
well as carrying Dad's. Well, there's me at the end of the
round sweating buckets, and he plops 25p in my hand and
says, 'Buy yourself something nice, wee man'.

I didn't really mind, I expect he needed the dough to fill
his bulging stomach which protruded through his patriotic
tartan trousers and shirt. Anyway I used to enjoy listening to
them talk as they marched half a yard on to the greens, or
more likely into the woods where more than one ball had
been lost. Usually it was either golf talk ('I've still not quite
got that swing right, Alex, I seem to have pulled it into the
lake'), or money talk. Always going on about how cuts were
having to be made at the office, due to bad times. I remained
sceptical, especially when they started discussing the
possibilities of buying a video recorder for Christmas. Alex,
though, never talked of his family, even though it was pretty
obvious they were close. I expect he didn't want to bring up
the subject of happy family life with Dad, and Dad never
seemed to talk about things like that at the best of times. I
know I never asked Dad about the break-up, maybe you

had more luck. Not that you seemed to, Karen. He'd pop you on his knee and clown around instead. You were always treated like the little toddler that he must have loved so much.

After our lunch at the bar, we'd go fishing or boating, which Ed enjoyed. He loved the boats, Karen, even if he couldn't row properly. And that was about it; the hours went by and 7.30 was soon arriving.

But this Sunday was different. Instead of having a drink at the bar with Alex and his lady, Dad told us we would be having a full meal that day.

'I've got someone special for you to meet; so Edward, I want you to be on your best behaviour.'

Well, Ed hadn't a clue what was going on but I knew it would be a 'lady-friend'. I wasn't expecting Jill, though, more a slightly greying, late forties widow-type that you meet at dinner parties. And when I saw this young dolly-bird I was really amazed. She was really good-looking that day, radiant with her Swiss-style hair on top of her head and a summer dress with blue spots on. She didn't look much older than you, Karen.

'Boys, I'd like you to meet Jill.'

I must have stared.

'Hi, lads,' she said.

'Hi,' I said, nudging Edward to say the same.

'Hello,' he said playing with his Rubic cube, which was like his replacement for a teddy bear.

'Your father's spoken a lot about you two.'

'He hasn't said much about you,' I said aggressively. Sometimes I was about as tactful as a hippo with constipation. Of course, you know that facet of my personality only too well. I never was the true gentleman was I, Karen? I'm working on it, though.

She laughed tentatively at my rudeness. I expect she was petrified of meeting us.

'Well folks, let's sit down,' Dad suggested, putting his hand into hers as reassurance while they led the way through to the very posh restaurant behind the main bar.

11

Ed turned to me, his blond hair all messed up over his face, like it always was. He's not changed, Karen.

'Who's she?'

'Sh..., it's his lady-friend.'

'Oh,' he said, like it didn't really matter and he started playing with his Rubic cube.

We settled in a pre-set table for four with me sitting opposite Jill and Ed beside me. It was real awkward.

'I thought it would be an idea for us all to get acquainted here because Jill's now an important part of my life.'

'Yeah, sure.'

'Jill and I are so close that we're getting engaged.'

He didn't beat about the bush. Straight out, no messing. You, being the over-sensitive type, might have totally flipped with the shock.

'Wow.'

'You're meant to say congratulations,' he said, rubbing his moustache with his finger like he did.

'Yes, terrific, I'm happy for you.'

'Oh, thank you,' said Jill.

'It's sort of ... sudden, well, what I mean is I didn't know you were involved.'

'That's because I didn't tell you, son. I wanted ... we wanted, to make sure it was on.'

'Does Karen know?' I asked, wondering whether he'd dropped it on you.

'Yes.'

'And Mum?'

He fiddled with his moustache.

'Yes, your mother knows.'

Another silence.

'We're hoping that you'll be looking on Jill as someone you can talk to as well.'

'Shall we order, dear?' Jill said very quickly.

'Yeah,' said Edward gleefully. He hadn't a clue what we'd been talking about. Well, maybe that's not true, but he hadn't quite grasped what had been said. Perhaps that's for the better.

By the time we got on to the dessert we were discussing Jill's life-story. A real classic, Karen. I half expected Eamonn Andrews to burst out of the kitchens and rush up to our table saying, 'Jill Dolly-bird, this is yer loif'.

'Jill works at the *Gazette*, you know,' Dad revealed.

'Oh yes?'

'She's a journalist.'

'Oh, what kind?' I said, trying to seem interested.

'The sort that writes.'

'No, what subject do you write on?'

'Oh sorry,' she giggled again and swallowed her portion of apple pie before answering. 'I do general work. Reporting on fêtes and interviewing local people. Pretty boring, I'm afraid.'

'Sounds OK.'

'Dad,' chipped in Ed pathetically, 'I want to go to the toilet.'

'I'll take him,' I said, happy to have a rest from talking to her. Not that I didn't like her, just that it was difficult making conversation. Well honestly, Karen, what lad my age could talk his way out of a situation like that? We left that stuff to you girls. That's why I was annoyed you weren't there. Here we were being introduced to our new stepmother, while you were light years away, probably at some intellectual orgy. I resented that.

Jill was all right, I guess. A little pushy maybe. It did seem strange, though, Dad and her together. After that I never thought of Dad the same way. I know I shouldn't have, but in a subconscious way I'd blamed Mum for the break-up; what with her nagging and that. Dad was always the one who took it in his stride and stayed calm when we played up. You remember, Karen. But after him and Jill, I'm having to rethink because now he's well set up and she's on her own.

Can you believe it all happened nearly three years ago? That day when we got back from school and they sat down at the table and told us how they were still friends but no longer loved each other. So brutally honest. And you cried for hours and hours. Boy, you shed some tears in your time,

13

Karen. I specifically recall you crying in your bedroom after they'd told us about the break-up. And I was next door, reading football books, totally without emotion. It was so distant and unreal for me.

And that last meal we had together. So quiet and weird, no one knew how to react. I thought he might come back, you know. Isn't it funny how the memories flood back? I've always blocked those moments out of my life.

After our meal at the golf club Dad took us all to some castle, which Ed thought was great but which bored me to tears. It took Ed an hour before he got tired of the place. He really had no concentration, did he? And then we went to the 'Olde Coffee Shop', an imitation of a real old coffee place, all timber and gas lamps. This was where the subject matter changed to good old me.

'How are you enjoying school?' Jill asked delicately, sipping her steaming coffee.

'I get by,' I replied with typical Jay Border enthusiasm. Well, what did you expect me to say? Lousy small talk again.

'What subjects are you taking?'

'English and History A levels.'

'Oh, tremendous,' she smiled, genuinely.

'Well, I wouldn't go that far.'

'Have you done any Shakespeare yet?'

'Yeah, we're doing Henry the somethingth.'

'Oh, I did Shakespeare at your age. I found it a real challenge. Not always easy to grasp but you could get your teeth into it. Oh yes, I used to have some tremendous tussles with him.'

'Must have been fun for Shakespeare.'

'Oh, you cheeky . . .' she slapped me gently like you birds do, with your hands all slack. As she touched me, I instinctively shook, like I didn't want her to touch me. It wasn't intentional.

'You won't get much out of him,' sneered Dad. 'They're

all apathetic at his age. All they care about is booze, birds and soccer. Nothing else matters. Right, son?'

'If you say so, Dad.'

'I expect he's got his eye on some girl,' said Jill.

'No way,' I defended.

'Funny you should say that, Jill, because, as it happens, I was at a business do at the Grand Hotel the other night and one of the people I spoke to was Mr Kirk, Penny's father.'

'So?'

'So she's been mentioning you by name.'

'Penny?'

'Yes, apparently you're in two of her classes. Very nice girl.'

A little hint from Dad that perhaps I should ask her out. Terrific, he runs off with some dolly-bird and then suggests how I should be running my love life. I got this feeling that Dad was expecting me to enter into some heavy relationship with a girl. After all, I was 'sixteen going on seventeen' and you'd been through some steady dates by then. Come to think of it, you'd gone with half the male population of Britain by then. Just a joke, Karen! Don't take it to heart. Actually, I expect he was secretly worrying that I was bent or uninterested. What would he know if I was? Anyway, at the time I didn't want to get into anything deep, I wanted it all casual. Why should I get serious, I thought, I've got time. I could hardly have expected how that sort of attitude would alter.

Penny was OK. Good-looking, bright, intelligent and she had good taste because she fancied me! I suppose I fancied her a touch and I don't mind people spreading rumours, it does things for your self-esteem. The time when I really sussed it out that she fancied me was one breaktime at school when she stormed towards our mob who were sat by the coats and lockers. In her hand was a poster she'd put on the notice board. Stone crazy on posters she was, whether they were on saving animals, or protesting about nuclear arms or what have you. Always one for a good cause was Penny. Which is all very nice, except that on the bottom of every poster it would say 'For more information contact Penny Kirk 6C, O.B.E., B. Sc., wonder woman, etc.' I guess you could have sympathised with her type, you weren't a poster freak, but you were crazy on sponsored things. Hell, it didn't have to be walks. It could be sponsored singing, eating, talking (you did well on that one) or anything. I had fun laughing at you for that.

Penny was breathing fire that day.

'OK, which one of you wise guys did this?'

She held up a poster which said broadly, in black print, 'DO YOU WANT A NUCLEAR HOLOCAUST?' and some kid had written below it 'yes, please'. Not exactly a major crime, but Pen was not amused.

'None of us,' said Carl, so innocent.

'I don't believe that, it's pretty plain that this remark has been made by someone with a low IQ, so it has to be one of you lot.'

'Must be Cookie,' said Justin.

'No chance.'

'Jay.'

'Leave me out of this,' I said. 'My money's on Bones.'

We all looked toward Bones, and his look of guilt said it all. His frail, skinny body looked even more frail as Penny, pony tails and all, turned toward him.

'You!' she scowled.

He smiled timidly.

'Probably.'

'And you call this humour. Vandalising constructive posters.'

'Just a joke,' he blurted out, rubbing his hand through his dark hair.

'Is that all you lot are here for, jokes?'

We paused and then nodded.

'Gore's going to hear about this. It's going right to the top.' When she flipped, she really flipped. Does that remind you of anyone?

'Look, Penny, I'll tell you what. To make up for my sins I'll go on that women's rights march with you on Saturday.'

16

'I wouldn't go on a march with you if someone had a gun pointed at my head.'

We all thought this was great fun. Nothing like getting some lass like Penny or you all hyped up. But my joy turned to acute embarrassment as she set on me.

'Jason, surely you don't agree with these slobs. I thought you were different.'

Ah, what a thing to say, Karen. All the lads had a ball playing her up with cat calls and whistles.

'Well . . .'

'Yes?' I felt the pressure on me to say something real diplomatic.

'I'm waiting.'

'I wouldn't get too upset, Penny. Take it as a joke.'

'You're not any better than them. Well, you are a bit I suppose, but you disappoint me.'

She walked away in disgust, her pert legs strutting.

'Well, that was fun,' said Marshall.

'Great fun,' I said. 'She hammered me.'

'Ah, but she fancies you, Jay. It's more than a rumour now. Did you see the love in her eyes?' They were laying it on thick this time. Putting me through it, they were.

'Come off it. She detests me,' I defended myself.

'I wouldn't say that, eh, Carl. Looked like love.'

'Oh, definitely.'

'And the way she stuck out her boobs when she was talking to you,' added Marshall, always the first to notice these things.

'Knock it off, lads.'

'What's the matter, Jay? Is Penny too trendy and dominant for you? I expect you prefer the more reliable type, those who'll cook and clean for you, the loyal housewife,' needled Carl, who loved stirring.

'That's right, Carl,' I said, refusing to bite, and I moved towards my next lesson on the upper block, lugging my books with me. Carl followed.

'You could do worse,' he said trying to slow me down. 'She's intelligent, interesting and she's got b. . .'

17

'I know. She's got big tits.'

'How coarse of you,' he smiled, revealing his slightly crooked teeth. 'I was about to say she had a lively personality. Think of those meaningful hours you could spend discussing the merits of unilateral disarmament or the role of women in society.'

Of course I denied liking her, I always did deny things until I wanted everyone to know the truth. I didn't even confide in you until I was positively sure about a girl. As it turned out, Penny dropped out of my life. Hey, Karen, it would have been easier if I'd have ended up going out with her. Soon I wasn't to give her, or any other bird, another thought.

THREE

Relaxation was getting home from school, heating up a cup of coffee and listening to my records. Of course this harmony was all too often broken by either Ed or Mum. My room has got even better since you left, Karen, even messier than before. A small and compact hole in a very organised mess. All my clothes were there somewhere, it was finding them that became difficult. Usually they were behind the hi-fi or on top of the bookcases or on the window ledge along with dozens of other things. Come to think of it, clothes could be found anywhere except in the drawers, which were almost totally obscured by newspapers or books. Not a room to win any competitions, but it did look lived in. You couldn't deny that point. Anyway, when important people came round I did tidy the place up, by chucking everything under the bed! No one knew ... except maybe you.

It was on a Tuesday, I think, that Mum asked me to go to the supermarket; yes, I'm sure because I remember I'd had six lessons that day and was shagged out. She was back early from work that day, earlier than I had expected. I hadn't peeled the potatoes and when I heard her come up the stairs I could sense trouble. As she entered I saw the tension clearly on her forty-year-old face. The age lines were obvious to see, even though they'd been partly hidden by make-up and face powder. She does look older, Karen, as though she's visibly aged since you left. There were even one or two grey hairs among the black. Not that she isn't still attractive, in an almost ice-cold, mysterious way (like that bird in the chocolate adverts). She's still as vain as ever and all, I tease her about it now and then. Of course, she hasn't got you to stick up for her now. Oh, Karen, those contact lenses she bought give her a hell of a lot of trouble, but she still wears them, even though I tell her she looks fine in glasses.

'Look at this room,' she said in that low-pitched, intense voice, as she half tripped over one of my shoes.

'It's all right.'

'And it smells, open that window, honey, and switch that music down.'

'Yes, Ma'am.'

'I'm expecting improvements in this room, Jason. Edward's room looks tidier than this tip,' she complained, picking up one of my T-shirts. Always obsessed with everything being perfectly in place; it was one of those things that she was barmy about. I guess all mums are barmy about something or other. You've got to agree on that one, Karen.

'I thought you were going to peel the potatoes,' she nagged on.

'Yes ... I was about to ... after this record was done.'

'Look, honey, you can fool some of the people some of the time but you can't fool your mum any of the time.'

I chuckled. She didn't miss too many tricks, did she?

'Well, I'll forgive you the potato peeling if you'll do me a favour tomorrow.'

'What favour?' I asked suspiciously.

'I've got Audrey and Harvey coming for a meal tomorrow and I'd like you to buy some steaks.'

'Who are Audrey and Harvey?'

'Oh, friends from the shop, you'll enjoy the company. They're great fun. Audrey is my assistant and her husband Harvey is a very successful businessman, in the underwear business.'

'Must be uplifting for him.'

'Now, Jason, you won't let me down. I could always rely on Karen to be a good host, always very courteous and helpful.'

There she went again, depicting you as some sort of heroine who never did any wrong. Not how I remembered you, but there you go. Don't get the wrong idea, Karen, you

20

were right more often than not. Thinking back, you were practically always right. What got me was how she portrayed you as Jesus Christ in order to make me feel guilty. That's a fair enough thing to say, isn't it?

As she was getting purple with rage, I told her I'd get the steaks. Oh sure, that only takes an hour of my time up after a hard day at school, I thought. And the shops in the town centre were about ten to fifteen minutes walk in the wrong direction, so I wasn't over-thrilled by the prospect. But I was glad I got those steaks, Karen.

Carl told me he'd come along to the supermarket after school so at least I had company. We went to the big place on the High Street by the flicks. Come to think of it, I hadn't been in there before. You were always the assistant shopper to Mum. That was your scene.

Now I expect you're thinking that world-shattering events don't usually happen in supermarkets. Well, smart-ass, you're wrong because one happened to me that day. Carl and I were approaching the now famous delicatessen corner, and it had loads of meaty stuff, sausages, coleslaws, cheese, and also two girls.

'Look at those two,' Carl pointed to the dames behind the counter as our trolley went that way. We didn't really need a trolley, but they're a good laugh and besides you might see one of your enemies and accidentally-on-purpose drive it into them. Terribly immature, huh? I got to doing stupid things with Carl, he was that sort of kid, had a sort of infectious stupidity. I got on well with Carl until recently; he was genuine, you knew what he was thinking. Wasn't all twisted like most. Oh, you only disliked him because he said you had a big arse. He was only being stupid on that one; 'immaturity' again, I guess.

These two girls were about our age, only one looked slightly older. Blonde hair, almost certainly bleached, good figure and a ton of make-up. But it was the other one I noticed. I knew that first time I saw her that she was special. She was smaller and gentler looking, beautiful eyes, dark, thick-set hair, just washed, I could tell. She wore one of those blue overalls that they all wear at these places as well as one of those daft paper hats. But she was still great, Karen, she hypnotised me, I'm not kidding, like hardly anyone could have done.

'Which one of those d'you fancy?'

'You what?' I said, looking at this girl.

'Which of those on the delicatessen counter do you fancy?'

I pretended not to have given it a second thought.

'Oh, I don't know.'

'The blonde's tasty, ah, do you get it? Tasty as in the food that you sell at the delicatessen.'

'Uh?'

'Never mind. But she ain't bad, that blonde. Seven on the Richter Scale. You know, I'm sure I've seen her before.'

'Oh, I prefer the other one, she looks nice,' I said in an almost distant way.

'Nice,' he shouted embarrassingly, his comic face screwing up, and then he whispered, 'How the hell do you know whether she's nice or not? Just because she isn't wearing black stockings and a red low-cut dress doesn't mean she's nice. For all you know, Jay, she may have slept around. Might be a tart ... probably is.'

'Well, cheers for telling me, Carl. That's really useful. The next time I want advice on the possibility of a bird being a pro I'll ask you.'

It was typical of him, Karen. One minute we were just looking at a couple of birds and the next he's telling me about the birds and bees.

You know, I'm sure I've seen that blonde before,' he continued. 'At a party, I think.'

'I doubt it.'

'I'll ask her.'

And he did, he always had the confidence to talk to anyone he wanted. He was one of these people that wasn't particularly good-looking (in fact he had crooked teeth and a broken nose) or even very nice but he had total confidence in himself. And that was his secret.

'Excuse me,' he said to this blonde as she wiped her hands, 'have I seen you somewhere before, I mean at a party?'

She stood there dumbfounded and said nothing for several seconds. Then she looked at the bird I fancied and started laughing, and the other one laughed as well. Poor Carl didn't know what to do, he went all red.

This blonde was really busting a gut, but when she finally stopped she said calmly, 'I've never ever seen you in my life.'

'Honest?'

'Honest.'

We walked away, with Carl muttering words to the effect that he was sure he'd seen her, although it was pretty obvious he'd got mixed up. And for some reason I looked back at the brunette that I'd liked, and our eyes met. And for what must have been a couple of seconds we looked at each other. And she was terrific, Karen. I was hooked from that moment on.

This romantic little incident was interrupted by an unromantic accident in which I crashed my trolley into some housewife, knocking two tins of pineapple chunks out of her hands. As Carl picked up the tins off the floor for her (which he did not do out of the kindness of his heart but because he fancied this woman, who was youngish) I decided that I might just be back to that delicatessen place before long. It was such a casual way to start what was to become the most important event in my life. How did you and Simon start? I figure that even you two must have begun like this. I bet you fancied him at first, but not deep love. Somehow after that glimpse of her I knew it would spiral. Was it the same for you, Karen?

Well, Audrey and Harvey weren't my cup of tea as far as people are concerned. But then I did have them to thank in an indirect sort of way for seeing this supermarket girl.

One of the troubles with you and Dad having left is that I

have to play joint host for Mum when she has these guests round. I'm the gentleman who takes their coats and pours them sherries. Can you picture how silly I felt?

You'll be amused to hear that Audrey described me as 'positively delicious', like I was a piece of chocolate cake. Very extravagant was Audrey, with everything, except for her hair. You see she was almost a skinhead, well, maybe not that bad, but it was short. She wore this flowery dress and a whole array of bracelets and rings. I expect she must keep some lucky jeweller going, with the amount she buys. A very extravagant talker as well, lovey-dovey talker. You'd have laughed, Karen. She was like Auntie Dot. Harvey was a foil for her, pretty quiet, an executive type, middle-aged with a nice suit and tie.

The worst part of the evening was when all four of us were sipping our sherries (yes, we'd managed to get Ed off to bed) and then Mum says, 'Oh, I must check the meal,' leaving me to small-talk with a panties salesman and his freak wife. What a predicament, I hear you say. I suppose I should have asked them about their hobbies. Oh no, she might have bored me with badminton talk or flower arranging.

'Would you like a cheesy football?' I said nervously, desperately trying to think of something more enlightening to say.

'Oh, no thank you.'

'Where are your brother and sister tonight?'

'My brother's in bed and Karen's at University.'

'Oh, how interesting,' said Audrey, sipping her sherry. 'She must be very intelligent.'

I grudgingly agreed, though I could have said you were a dunce and had got into Durham by cheating during exams. Don't panic, I was very polite about you.

'What is she doing there, Jason?'

'A degree course in psychological studies, I think.'

'Ah ... how awfully interesting. I suppose she'll be learning about sex maniacs like Freud. He was a psychiatrist of some sort, wasn't he, Harvey? I don't suppose Jason will have studied him yet.'

'Yes, I have a bit.'

'Oh, jolly good. It's amazing what they teach nowadays.' I hadn't a clue what she was on about. Sounded like verbal diarrhoea to me, but who am I to say?

'Our Jeremy is currently doing an A level course, you know. But he's doing the more practical studies such as mathematics and the physical sciences.'

'Oh.'

'Yes, he's working very hard at the moment.'

That was probably a lie, I expect he was a dosser really, but Audrey wouldn't be the kind to admit that sort of thing.

'What school does Jeremy go to?' I asked. Excellent small talk on my part, don't you think? By now I was egging her on.

'He goes to Trentwood Valley,' said Harvey, at last getting a word in.

'The place on the other side of town, Jason,' butted in Audrey. 'On the whole a nice school, but it tends to take in some children from inner city areas, so that the classes are mixed.'

'What, boys and girls?'

'No dear, blacks and whites. Not that the blacks are too bad, most of them are really very nice; but it does slow down the class when some children get behind.'

'Must be tough for Jeremy,' I said tongue in cheek. This old girl was really cracking me up inside, a real case. I thought her sort of prejudices had disappeared in the middle ages.

'Luckily for Jeremy he's a strong-willed young man,' she continued, 'isn't he, Harvey?'

'Yes dear,' he replied.

And then, thankfully, Mum called us up for the meal before I could turn the conversation on to the subject of poor Harvey's underwear business.

FOUR

'What's your opinion on that?' asked the young and pretty Miss Turner as she looked towards me uncompromisingly along with twenty other gawping teens. Who did you have for English, Karen? It wasn't Turner, was it? I think it was that Mr Ray, who picked his nose. I seem to remember you two had a personality clash. Poor bloke, he's probably still recovering. Well, he may have been a jerk, but she was on the ball, really into teaching. She'd sussed out that I'd been day dreaming and hadn't been listening to what was going on. I'd practically fallen asleep, to be honest with you; not that the lesson was boring but the room was dead stuffy and warm, with the sun from one of the windows catching me and burning me up.

'Opinion, who to?'

'What's your view on Henry's motives towards Falstaff in this scene?'

I was really in it, Karen. My mind had mysteriously wandered away from Henry the bloody fifth. And don't try and tell me that you actually enjoyed reading that stuff.

I had to make something up.

'Well, Miss Turner ... my views are exactly the same as yours. I really have nothing to add to your comments.'

I couldn't understand why I heard people sniggering at me.

'Good try, Jason. The only thing was that it wasn't me talking, it was Janice who was making the point.'

I looked up into the air for inspiration.

'Sorry,' I murmured pathetically. 'I wasn't listening.'

'No, Jason, I rather gathered that,' she said in her

teacher's voice. 'Well, do try to pay a bit more attention in future if you can.'

'Sure.'

I looked down at my notes, pretending to be concentrating dead hard, even though I was still recovering from the embarrassment of being hammered in front of the whole class. I guess this sort of thing never happened to you, so you wouldn't know the feeling.

'OK, class. On that less than auspicious note we'll end the lesson for today. Now just remember that essay for Friday; minimum, five hundred words. No excuses, please, you've had a month to work through it. Thank you.'

Everyone got up and there was the noise of dragging chairs on the floor as Justin and I left the room together.

'Oh Jason, could you hold on a minute? I'd like a word with you.'

The softness of the teacher's voice was only just loud enough to catch my attention. Hers was a very soft, gentle voice like on those washing-up ads. You see how many adverts I still watch on the telly. I can remember loads off by heart now, Karen. I bet I can do more than you now. Was that a stupid pastime, or what?

Miss Turner continued, 'I only want a little word.'

'Yeah, OK.'

'You're in it now, son,' muttered someone.

'Beginning of the end,' someone else added.

'I don't know, I wouldn't mind having a few heart to hearts with Miss Turner. She's all right,' Justin argued.

I ignored the comments around me. I was too interested in what she was going to say. I wasn't nervous or anything, but I did wonder what she wanted. As you know, it was sort of typical for me to get into this sort of hassle. It wasn't as if I was extra naughty or got into scraps, but I always got into trouble for talking or not concentrating.

'I'll be with you in a minute, Jason.'

Keely Wigan was speaking to Miss Turner as she always seemed to at the end of lessons. Come to think of it, she did practically everything bar give Miss Turner an apple to get her attention. She was the sort that was extra friendly with teachers, 'a happy working relationship with the members of staff' you might say. I guess you had a few Keely Wigans at university.

'Oh, Miss Turner, have you got any more paper? I've used up my supply,' she drawled in her soppy voice. 'Yes sir', 'no sir', 'three bags full sir', Keely's own ever so clever way of letting teacher know that she was working her very hardest. That was all that annoyed me about Keely; she was quite sweet and friendly, but what a creep.

'I'll give out the paper at lunch-time, Keely. I'm a bit pushed for time right now.'

'Fine, I'll see you, Miss Turner.'

'Goodbye, Keely.' She smiled pleasantly and then started talking to me.

'Do you need some more paper, Jason?' she joked.

'Um, not yet, thanks.'

She got straight to the point.

'Look, Jason, I haven't come here to tell you off. It isn't really our job in the Sixth Form, or it shouldn't be. I'm a little concerned, though, about your general approach. You don't seem to be putting your all into it.'

'No.'

'I wondered whether you were having any problems. You know that there are loads of people you can talk to.'

'No, everything's fine.'

She smiled again, unconvinced. I felt as if she could see right through me. Some people can do that, can't they, Karen?

'It's the boredom of the lessons, Miss. Not that your lessons are bad.'

'I understand. You know, I was your age once.'

I believed her, she was the believable sort. A real genuine person.

'Try and look on it as a job, Jason, a target. Once you've got your A levels you can do what you want, maybe you'll find something you enjoy.'

'Yeah, I guess.'

She started to get all her books together, indicating that she was going out of the room.

'OK, Jason. That's all. Thank you.'

She was thanking me, Karen. Wow, that was nice. I remember the days when we used to have lectures from teachers at our old schools. They'd knacker you for nothing, talking about your lack of discipline and what a disgrace to society you were. But at least at those places you had someone to blame for your frustrations, so that if you felt depressed you could blame it on the teachers. At this level, all of a sudden you've officially changed from a kid to a student. And everyone's so appallingly pleasant even if they hate your guts. And that's even worse, because in the end you get to wondering whether the genuine ones like Miss Turner are really phoneys like the rest. OK, so that may sound bull to you, Karen. I'm not proud of it, but it's the way I think.

I walked out of the classroom expecting to be the centre of attention but to my surprise hardly anyone noticed me. All the lads were huddled together on the table by the careers office gossiping about one thing or another. No one saw me.

'Hey, am I missing out on something here?' I asked.

'Bones is taking bets,' answered Marshall, combing his hair as usual.

'What on?'

'A couple of things. He's giving 3-1 odds on Liverpool winning the League.'

'Must be mad. They'll easy win it. I'll take him on for that.'

'You think Liverpool will win the League?'

'Yeah,' I said, 'with their midfield, and they've got strength in depth.'

I always pretended to be a football expert, although to be truthful I never went any more. Gone were the days when I went to matches, leaving you and Mum in spasms of anxiety about how I was going to get beat up. I don't bother now, got better things to do, but I still pretend to be into football, because it's a big talking point.

I was discussing the finer points of the game with the lads when John Curtis came steaming down the corridor as if World War III had been announced. He was dying to tell us something, I wondered what it was.

'Get this lads, Cookie's going out with a bird.'

'You're kidding?'

'No, I'm not. It's true.'

'Who'd go out with him?' said Marshall, all cocky.

'Jeanie Wood.'

'Not the Jeanie Wood in his maths class with the droopy eyes and double chin?' laughed Carl, all ready to hammer other people for their looks despite his own.

'Yeah, that's the one,' said John, totally out of breath with excitement.

'Shit, she ain't exactly one of nature's beauties,' said Bones; a boy that resembled an anaemic rake, he was one of those lanky kids who looked underfed even though he ate all the time. Just think, Karen, if you'd have been like that you could have eaten normal food without going all neurotic. When I think of you eating all that spinach and asparagus and celery, it makes me laugh. I think I'd rather have looked like Orson Welles than starve like you.

'You're not exactly Robert Redford yourself, Bones,' I noted.

'All right, Jay. Point taken. But don't tell me you like her.'

I said nothing for once. Me, speechless. I expect you find that unbelievable.

'I'd rather go with a wog,' said Justin. That was the ultimate horror for him. He hated blacks. I blame his parents for that, our roots would never have let us attack anyone like that. Do you remember that time ages ago, when we were watching Tarzan and I said, 'Mum, if he was born in the jungle, why isn't he a coon?' Straight to bed and no supper. Not surprising, I suppose, but that's about your average Sixth Form comment.

'I know the odd nigger girl who'd get upwards from five

30

on the Richter Scale,' said Bones. 'It's the dirt black ones that are ugliest, like Leona.'

I nearly stuck up for her, Karen, but decided it was pointless getting mad over it when I'd only be laughed at. There seemed no point, back then.

'Talking of bets, boys, I'll bet anyone that Cookie and his old gal won't last for more than a week. Have I got any takers?' said Bones.

Everyone went quiet. Not many took Bones on because he nearly always won. A deep one he was, he appeared as though he couldn't add two and two, but in reality he was a real boff. Behind all the smart chatter he was dead intelligent.

Call this the old Jay Border stupidness, or even call it nobility, but I had to stick up for Cookie in some way.

'I'll take you on. Cookie will last at least a month.'

I'm not sure whether I did it to stick up for Cookie or what.

'Bad bet,' smiled Bones wickedly. 'If I were you I'd put my money on Liverpool at 3-1 but on the other hand if you want to be charitable I'll give you the bet at 4-1 odds.'

'You're on. 25p at 4-1.'

We shook hands firmly. I felt almost ridiculous.

'You twat.'

'You must be thick.'

'You'll see,' I said defiantly, but as I thought about it more I knew I'd most likely be on a loser.

Ah, but as if a 25p bet was all that important. There were more important things to fret about than that. That bird, you remember the one I was telling you about, well, I had to see her again, it was a sort of compulsion, I wasn't even sure at that time whether she meant that much to me. But I followed my instincts just this once.

The first time I spoke to her was when Ed and me were in town one day after school. I had to buy the kid some trousers which he needed, because he'd ruined his others falling in a bog (stupid chump). It was a real drag, Karen. I hate clothes shopping anyway but with a six-year-old half wit who said he hated every pair he put on it was torture. At about the sixth shop we tried I told him that if he didn't like the next pair I would buy them anyway, to spite him. So surprise, surprise, Ed decided that he liked these brown trousers and we eventually bought them.

And then I had this brainwave, which I have every now and again. We were real near the supermarket, so I decided to go in because I had to see this girl again. Of course Ed didn't want to go but I bribed him into coming by buying him a packet of jelly babies.

It was the first time I ever spoke to this girl properly, Karen, so you could understand that I was on edge.

'Now I'm going to get some ham,' I explained to Ed, using that excuse to go to the delicatessen.

'I don't want any ham,' he moaned, like he does, in his little kid voice.

'Well, I do. And if you don't shut up I'm going to nick all your jelly babies and stamp on them.'

That shut him up, thank goodness. A bit of discipline like you sometimes gave him often worked on the poor lad. He sucked his thumb in misery and pulled behind me.

I couldn't believe how nervous I was as I walked towards the delicatessen. I had to get a real grip of myself, because I was practically a wreck. It wasn't like me at all, I never got this churned up inside.

She was the only bird serving, the blonde number wasn't there. In the same outfit as before, as I remembered her.

'I'll have some ham, please,' I said trying to be really cool and sophisticated.

'What kind of ham, sir?' That was the first thing she ever said to me. I'd wondered for ages how she spoke and her voice was exactly like I imagined. It was a terrific voice, Karen, no kidding.

I didn't know what to say.

'What kinds have you got?'

She grinned.

'Quite a few kinds, this one here and the smoked here.'

I was finding it hard to concentrate on what she was saying.

'Oh, I don't know.' How appallingly indecisive I was. It was slipping by me too fast. I wanted to play the whole dialogue back. Perhaps I should have been more dominating and confident, do you think? Some sharp line like, 'Hey, honey lips, what's a sugar plum fairy like you doing in a joint like this?' OK, so that's ridiculous. Don't tell me, Simon chatted you up perfectly. I'll have to get some tips from him.

'What kind of ham do you recommend?'

'None of them. Buy the cheapest.'

'OK, I'll have the cheapest.'

'Good decision.'

She chuckled lightly and cut the ham on one of those gem cutting machines.

'That'll be 35 pence, sir.'

I handed the exact money over, and felt my hand gently touch hers as she took it. I'm sure she didn't notice. The whole thing was ruined by – guess who?

'Is that your brother?' she remarked.

I looked behind me, puzzled at the question. To my horror I saw Ed pulling apart one of these cheese exhibitions, the sort that plops lumps of Dutch Edam on paper plates, with flags stuck in them. Not doing things by halves either, he was literally pulling all the plates off the neatly set tables. How, Karen, could a kid so young destroy so much, in so little time? It's always in public as well. It was in the middle of a clothes shop that he puked up his lunch in that old dear's handbag.

It was panic stations, Karen. This snobby beauty queen with a sash saying 'Miss Cheese 1982' charged towards us, threateningly crying out, 'The kid's ruined it, the little bugger.' At first I froze, but my instincts soon took over. I dropped the ham and heaved Ed up by the waist and ran as hard as I could, passing surprised shoppers on the way.

When we were two hundred yards down the street I put

him down and paused for breath. He stood there looking so dopey, Karen, like he does. In his hand was a piece of cheese which he was nibbling. I started to laugh, it was so funny. It had been one of those afternoons.

FIVE

The loud, shrill noise of the school bell was music to my ears. Our lesson was over and it was lunch. Praise the Lord, I thought. There was the usual rush to get in the queue early and the narrow staircase was packed with pushing sixth-formers.

I was quite far up the queue in with Carl and a kid called Henry Mansfield. Of course I was mouthing it about how hungry I was. Ah yes, Karen, no diet foods for me. You keep your yoghurts and salads while I take fish and chips with apple pie for pudding.

'I could eat a horse,' I said.

'You may have to, the sort of stuff they dish out here.'

'Oh, I don't know. I reckon the food's all right.' I pointed to the battered blackboard ahead which showed the day's menu. 'Look, you've a choice of Hawaiian Grill, Spaghetti Al Forno and Chef's Surprise. Sounds good.'

'My young man, it may sound good but is it really nice or are they having you on?' said a voice.

I looked behind me to see the beaming face of Lenny Burton, Mr Popular, the type that knew everyone and was admired by everyone. What a creep and a bore. He was the kind that borrowed money off you and took half a year to pay it back. But then he was popular, and his sort think they can get away with murder. You'd been out with a few carbon-copies of Lenny before you met Simon. They're all the same.

'Hi, Lenny,' I acknowledged.

'My friend (he always referred to me as "my friend" or "my young man"), observe the menu. In reality Hawaiian

Grill is bacon and egg with a piece of pineapple on top and what do you think Chef's Surprise is?'

'Don't know.'

'Meat stew, and what, young man, is the surprise?'

'Give up, Lenny.'

'There isn't any meat in it.'

Funny boy is Lenny.

'Hey, Jay,' he asked, moving on to a new subject. 'Have you finished with my album?' I'd borrowed his Black Sabbath record a week before, not that I liked it all that much but it's how we lads socialise.

'Nearly finished with it.'

'Have you been listening to it then?'

'Yeah, of course,' I lied. I never did lie very convincingly, did I, Karen? It made me blush a bright shade of red.

'What track did you like best?'

Now that was a difficult question to answer seeing as I hadn't listened to any of the tracks; so I took a guess.

'The third track on the first side was good,' I said hopefully.

'You jerk,' he squalled viciously, showing his white teeth to all. 'Hey lads, listen to this. My mum was listening in and she said she liked that one.'

Well, Karen, let's face it; if you were going to be one of the lads, it simply wasn't on for your mum to like your type of music. Very un-cool, a real crime. Against the rules, that, and us morons had to follow the rules, didn't we? Let's try and work it all out.

Rule 1 – We've already discussed rule 1, but it's crucial. So pay attention, girl. Do not agree with mummy and daddy. Come to think of it, you shouldn't be in agreement with anyone over the age of thirty, because people are 'past it' at thirty according to the younger generation. Penalty for disobedience – rejection.

Rule 2 – Very important this rule is. It involves the type of music that you simply have to like. Now there is a choice for you here. You can choose to pose as a heavy metal fan liking loud and rebellious music. If this does not suit your own individual taste you can turn to new wave which is (how can I describe it?) loud and rebellious; then there is mod music which is not so loud and rebellious.

This particular group of sixth-formers will not allow you to like disco music (horror of horrors), middle of the road, ballads or classical. Sorry, Karen, you birds who go for that stuff are in deep trouble, as penalty for disobedience is rejection once more. Not that you'd lose sleep over the 'boys' rejecting you. I'm sure you wouldn't have had it any other way. That doesn't mean it wasn't important to me. All that heavy, loud stuff I played on my stereo; it drove you crazy. But I had to choose it, you must see that, because believe it or not everyone else liked it as well.

Rule 3 – We sixth formers are obsessed with looking for some sort of identity to fit in with the group. Even you were guilty of following this one, Karen. You were perfect in the role of trendy yet intelligent girly. You lot were the bourgeoisie of the school.

Taking the 'morons', the 'poorer relations' you might say, our image was that of rockers (requirements being long hair, preferably not washed for weeks so that it's all greasy, and denim clothes with metal badges).

Now, Karen, to project this image, we 'lads' must have an attitude to go with it. This brings us to a very important aspect of Rule 3: to become popular within our group it is essential to be a rebel against society's nasty little values like being nice to people or caring for others. You must remain cool and casual with a 'couldn't care less' view of everything around you.

Oh, and another rule I nearly forgot, Karen. It helps if you are a heavy drinker. ('Hey man, you haven't lived until you're pissed' sort of thing.) Being a smoker helps as well because we don't care, you know, if we die of lung cancer, because we don't care about anything.

Well, I followed the rules to the dot. I drank, I smoked and I pretended to like heavy metal music. At the same time, whilst I was reasonably intelligent, my attitude to work was laissez-faire. And so I was a fully pledged and accepted member of the group of sixth formers commonly known as 'the lads', and what a bunch of asterisks we all were. You don't have to tell me that, Karen.

Now of course, there were those brave or sensitive enough to do their own thing. But they couldn't win because they were unpopular except with a few of their own kind. 'Classical musicians' were thought of as Martians (as were disco freaks). Then, last but not least, there was the dying breed of middle of the road kids like Adam who listened to Leo Sayer and Gilbert O'Sullivan at the beginning of the year, but strangely and (just perhaps not coincidentally) their tastes were altered to the heavy metal sound. That makes me sad when I think of it.

Lenny was the typical sixth former in my eyes. He had the manner and smile that made you want to throw up. But I mustn't be too rude, because he was my official friend even if he did probably detest me.

As we moved along the lunch queue gathering our stew and chips he'd be chatting away, if not to us, then to the pretty dinner lady who served vegetables. 'Is there any chance of double portions?' he said.

We finally got all our grub and carried our trays over to the table nearest the window where Justin and Bones were sat. We always claimed that table if we could, we tried to reserve certain parts of the school at breaks and dinner. We informally owned them in a way. Everyone did it, you girls seemed to reserve the parts of the school furthest away from us. I wonder why!

As we sat down, gobbling our food, Lenny spoke yet again.

'Listen in, lads,' he moved in close to us, whispering. 'I've some grass.'

I wasn't listening. My thoughts were totally concentrated on the dinner plate. You really upset me when you cracked that I should never take a girl to a candlelight meal, because I'd be doing too much eating.

38

Most of the others were totally engrossed in what Lenny was on about.

'Same stuff as last time?' asked Carl.

'Same stuff, same price and available now.'

'I'll take some. A fiver's worth. That's all I can afford,' Carl whispered.

'Same here,' said Bones, sitting next to me with his mouth full of chips.

I butted in, eager to find out what all the tension was about.

'Excuse me, lads, but can you get me in on your wavelength?'

'Shut up, Jay. Keep your voice down,' said Lenny, all panicky and looking around anxiously, even though it was pretty obvious that no one was taking a blind bit of notice of what he was saying.

'Sorry I spoke,' I apologised sarcastically. More sarcasm, huh?

'Dope!' Carl stated as if he was losing his patience.

'I know I'm a dope, but there's no need to get all annoyed.'

'You wet mop. The stuff Lenny's selling is dope. As in m-a-r-i-j-u-a-n-a, also known as pot.'

'Oh, that kind of dope,' I sighed.

'Shhh.'

'Sorry,' I said, dead quiet, and I put my finger over my mouth.

'Well, Border,' said Lenny, all authoritatively, 'do you want any?'

I should have said nothing at that moment. I know that, Karen, but I always do the not so smart thing.

'I've never had it, so I don't know what it's like.'

'Hey man, it's crazy stuff. Good stuff, I mean.'

At last I stopped eating. You should have seen everyone staring at me. All of a sudden, I felt myself in deep water.

'Have you had it, Carl?'

I was hoping he'd say no.

'Yeah, sure.'

'Justin?'

'Not yet but I'm buying some this time round. You ought to join me.'

'No, it's not my scene.'

I started eating again, hoping that that would be the end of it. But they kept on at me, Karen, they were talking about it the whole time.

'It's not hard stuff, Jay,' said Lenny. 'Harmless stuff, it's like being under sedation; you feel all light and good, but you're not sure what's happening. It's real crazy. There's no need to be scared of it, Jay.'

'I'm not,' I said defiantly.

'I know that,' he answered. 'Do you want some?'

I thought for a second.

'Yeah, go on.'

'How much do you want?'

'Only enough for a try.'

'I'll give you a fiver's worth then.'

'Yeah, OK.'

'My friend, you won't regret it.'

He smiled his phoney smile. But I did regret it, Karen. I felt almost guilty. I know it wasn't like the films where you've got some guy in a pin-striped suit and a small polythene bag pushing it around. But I'd still sworn I'd never get into drugs, ever since that T.V. programme we'd seen years back on heroin addicts. How you showed off about when you refused marijuana cookies at some wild party that you went to. Hell, you were right again, always bloody right.

He gave me the stuff later that day. A minute quantity, didn't look like anything much. He told me not to flash it around and not to get stoned before school (as if I was going to). And he also told me to enjoy it, which I never did. I hadn't the guts to refuse it, and I hadn't the guts to take it.

You'll think this funny, Karen, but I had it nicked that afternoon. Is that ironic or what? I think the stars had predicted a rewarding day so that just goes to prove that they're one big con.

I went into town that afternoon, on my own. I should have gone to football practice but I was really depressed about the dope. I often went into town after school (when Edward was being looked after by neighbours, that is). Increasingly I went in on my own and I'd hang around the amusement arcade and play a few games on the invaders machines. Those machines didn't half suck my money up. Another thing for you to disapprove of, huh? 'You fritter your money away, Jay' – that comment would be typical. But then you frittered your dough on expensive clothes. So there!!!

So I was playing this invaders machine like I did quite often and then this incident happened. My mind was concentrated on this game because I was scoring dead well. 3500 I had, which was the third best I'd ever done. Well, you see, this kid came up beside me, I didn't look at him at first but I felt his presence.

He watched for a second.

'Hey boy, you want to lend me some money?'

It was a West Indian accent and I looked round. He was a tall six-footer with one of those massive great woolly hats they wear. He was wearing casual clothes, a ski jumper and dossed up jeans, but he sure wasn't casual. I tried to ignore him.

'Hey boy,' he repeated, 'give me 10p. You wanna give me 10p?'

'I can't say I'm wild about the idea, mate,' I said breezily, trying to bring some humour into it. My dumb way of being nice. 'I've no money. All out. Sorry.'

He wasn't impressed. Just stood there looking mean.

'Look dude, I hears jangling in your pockets. Now I might not be brainy like you schoolboys but when I hears jangling I sees money.'

He knew I was a school kid which didn't augur well for me, I suppose, because I expect he was on the dole and blamed it on people like you and me.

'Well ... it is money in a way ... it's my bus fare.'

'Walk!'

'I couldn't do that,' I said nervously, still playing the machine. 'I live three miles outside.'

'Hey boy, I only want 10p.'

Have you ever tried playing the machine and talking to a kid who's about to break your legs at the same time? No, I don't think you've ever had that problem. Trust me when I tell you it's not easy.

'Will you leave off,' I stormed. 'That black kid over there's got plenty of money.'

He walked to this other kid on the other side of the arcade and I thought that was that. It wasn't thirty seconds, though, before they both came over, this other kid marching purposefully toward me, his hawk eyes looking straight at me.

'This is the boy, Leonard. He called you a black boy.'

'Schoolboys think they can say anything,' he said in a one-tone voice as if it was a struggle to speak.

He pulled me viciously away from the machine up to his face. He smelt of booze or something. He had sweat on his face and he snarled, it wasn't my imagination. Well, perhaps it was.

'That's a mean thing to say, schoolboy.'

'Yeah.'

'I ought to bust your ass, boy.'

He threw me down against the machine. I knocked my leg against the floor. I limped up, I was real angry. I'd been bullied way back at junior school by a nutter with buck teeth, who went by the name of Floyd. I never told anybody about that, you know. I figured that this was my day to become a super-hero.

Briskly, I moved towards the change counter before they could touch me.

'Um,' I cough to get the bloke at the counter's attention. He was reading a paper and smoking a cigar. He was a right dosser, unshaven and half undressed. Not the sort to turn you on. 'These two kids here are hassling and making trouble.'

'What, Winston and Leonard?' he exclaimed as if Winston and Leonard were the nicest kids you could ever hope to meet.

'Yeah, that's right.'

'Ah, don't worry about them. Just be nice to them and they're fine.'

They laughed. I was dumbfounded as the bloke went back to reading his paper and smoking his cigar.

'Is that it?' I asked, feeling more vulnerable and less brave than I had a few seconds earlier. Can you blame me, Karen?

'I'm not the cops, kid. If you don't like it here then get out.'

'I'll do that.'

I picked up my school-bag which was by the machine and started on my way out. I'd had enough of the place and I knew that if I valued my life I'd better skip. My friends Winston and Leonard weren't too impressed and, being the terrific guys they were, grabbed me just as I reached the doors.

One of them grabbed my neck, real hard it was. I felt his cold hand locked against the bone. I was scared, I'll admit it. I'm telling you, Karen, I thought he was going to kill me. All those dreams of me being a super-hero were vanished and I was plain scared stiff.

The other one picked my pockets, taking my money and keys. The bloke at the counter read his paper not more than fifty yards away. He must have seen me, Karen.

'How much he got, Leonard?'

'Not much,' said the other creep. 'About 50p. Hey, wait a minute.' He took out my sachet of dope and held it up to the light with glee on his face. 'He's got dope. I swears that this schoolboy's got dope.'

'Give me that,' said the other. 'Where d'you get this, schoolboy?'

'School.' I could hardly talk, Karen, I was breathless.

43

'You don't want this, schoolboy. You could get into trouble, man. I'll take it off your hands.'

I wasn't in the mood to argue.

'Hey, let him go, Winston. We got his dope.'

'Yeah.' This other kid let go of me gently, he still looked at me though. And then before I could blink he thumped me as hard as he could in my stomach. I cringed with the agonising pain, I couldn't stand up straight. 'Now, schoolboy; I don't want to see your face here again, you dig?'

I said nothing but stumbled away. I felt sick, Karen. I expect you'd say it was all I deserved for buying the dope. In a way you're right. But at that moment, I felt like I'd lost all my pride.

The only person I told (before you) about the incident was Carl. You see, he phoned me up that evening to tell me off about not turning up for football practice, and I arranged to meet at the Fox and Hounds so that I could tell him the whole story over a pint. We always went down the Fox and Hounds in the sixth form. It was like our headquarters, a good pub it was. They never checked to ask us our age and it was real posh furnishing and they had pool tables and bar football. You'd have thought it too pleasant for the 'morons'. It was more inhabited by people like you.

Carl wasn't too impressed with the whole story.

'You giant-sized KLUTZ,' he moaned. 'That's what you are.'

'What's a klutz?'

'You're a klutz, that's what.'

'I thought I was being pretty courageous, but there you go,' I sighed, disappointed at his response.

'Jay, in order to live a happy and successful life, don't drink, don't smoke and don't mess around with nutters in amusement arcades.'

There he was again, Karen. Telling me how to run my life. Yeah, occasionally he was bossier than you. I'd half

44

expected you to direct us by phone from the university. But you never did phone.

When Carl nagged, I changed the subject.

'You want a game of pool?' I said.

'Yeah.' We moved towards the pool table, it was a game he nearly always won. 'If Bones were here he'd put a bet on the game.'

I laughed. 'And he wouldn't bet on me.'

'Anyhow, it serves you right for missing football practice. No one knew where you'd got to.'

'Forgot.'

'Hell, Jay, I reminded you second last lesson.'

'OK, so I didn't want to know. Football's not my scene any more,' I remarked as I set up the pool balls.

'What are you on about? You were the one who said football wasn't a matter of life or death, it was much more.'

'I didn't say that. Some manager said it on TV.'

'Even so, you're changing your tune just lately.'

'Shut up, Carl, and play the game.'

'Jay, you're getting all weird,' he remarked, playing the opening shot of the pool game. In a way I realised he was right about my growing away from football. It wasn't planned.

'You know what I reckon, it's that dope. You're still high on it.'

'I've got other things to get high on,' I said, thinking of the supermarket girl. 'And anyway, I told you, it was nicked before I touched it.'

'Come again?' he said, his odd face all perplexed.

'Quiet. I'm playing my shot.'

This will come as a surprise to you. I hit the cue ball rather inaccurately and missed all the balls.

'See,' I said, 'you put me off.'

I lost the pool game.

SIX

I wonder whether old Mr Miller would've described me as a klutz; more likely he'd've called me a young hooligan. I expect he saw me as one of these football nuts that spent his spare time spraying graffiti on walls and lobbing bricks through windows.

He was a laugh, though. I didn't mind popping in to see him from time to time, even if he did prefer it when you looked after him. 'Where's your sister?' he'd ask hopefully, only to be saddened when I told him repeatedly that you were at university.

I went there every week practically, I'd pop in and make him a cup of tea. He'd go on about one thing or another, the neighbours, the price of a Mars bar and so on. The most uncomfortable bits were when he started reminiscing about old times. He'd get all emotional over his old dear and how things weren't the same without her. Or he'd worry about being carted away to a Home. I didn't know how to calm him down. What did you do, Karen?

He became a regular part of my routine, did Mr Miller. I even took him to the doctor's one afternoon, which I'll tell you about in a second. It was because of his legs which got all stiff and hard. I could tell it was causing him loads of trouble because I saw the pain on his face when there was strain on his legs. I asked him often about it, but he ignored me and when I finally got him to admit it was troublesome I advised him to see a doctor.

'I don't need a doctor,' he answered, getting his knickers in a twist.

'Well, why on earth not? They'll give you some help, Mr Miller.'

'I don't trust doctors,' he groaned, as he sat in his coffee-stained armchair by the old television. 'They're all so young now. I see them on these programmes and they're not many years past sixteen.'

'I'm young, Mr Miller,' I reminded him.

'Aye, that's what worries me.'

He shook his balding head and started sucking one of the mints that he's always got without fail.

'What's wrong with me?' I asked, probing his mind.

'No morals,' he cried out. 'When I was a nipper my parents would teach me order 'nd authority. I'd get the cane if I was caught picking apples in the local orchard.'

It was funny that he said picking and not stealing.

'And ...' I said, coaxing him on because he made me laugh when he carried on like this. Oh, Karen, he couldn't have been this cussed with you. I expect he thought you were sugar and spice.

'And now, all they'd do is stick you in one of these damn rehabilitation centres.'

'That's very interesting, Mr Miller, but what's this got to do with young doctors?'

That made him think. I observed him slowly sucking his mint as he searched for an answer.

'It's all about morals, young man. Where are all the morals?'

'Mr Miller, forget the morals. The doctors will give you some pills for your legs.'

'You're not grasping my point.' He was a stubborn old thing, never willing to accept a point or alter his views. Perhaps my patience level wasn't as high as yours, because I told him what I thought of all the bull he was churning out, finishing up with, 'Well, I give in. You're hopeless.'

Then to my amazement he spoke, only quite humbly this time.

'Jason.'

'Yes.'

'I'll go . . . but I'd be happier if you'd go with me.'

Victory. I felt like it was something of a compliment from a bloke who claimed I had no morals. I had that sort of smug, contented feeling that you get when you know that you're helping a guy who needs your help. I felt like some sort of a Samaritan, even if it was a petty favour. I suppose I felt so good because I didn't get the chance to help that often. It was more or less your life's work, helping practically everyone of some shape and size. I figured it was my turn.

The one thing that I was nervous about to do with visiting the doctor's was that the doc might notice my grazes and bruises from my little set-to with Winston and Leonard. What if he asked me how I'd got the marks? I didn't want to embarrass myself by admitting I'd been duffed in.

Strangely enough, it wasn't our local surgery, it was that place down Alton Road. Why Mr Miller went there and not to the nearest place remains a mystery, but I wasn't one to argue with him, not now I'd persuaded him to go.

And I'll let you into something else, Karen. If you ever want a laugh to cheer yourself up just pop down to the local waiting room at a doctor's or hospital. They're such a fun bunch that go there, always willing for a chat and a joke.

In our own exciting waiting room there were four people sat in the cramped but warm cubby hole. Most of those there were pretending to be engrossed in the *Woman's Own* or *Punch* mags which had been neatly set for everyone to read.

I sat in one of the wooden chairs, decrepit chairs at that, which were available. The room was depressing, it seemed old and there was a pessimistic atmosphere, if there is such a thing. And ahead of me was this clock on the wall and I promise that it was the most ordinary, boring clock I've ever seen in my short existence. No Mickey Mouse hands to cheer up the patients, but simple black lines and twelve numbers.

What a yawn. I watched the seconds go by but after I got to forty-three even that became boring.

So I decided to analyse the people in the waiting room instead. It was one of those daft games I played when boredom threatened to set in. It was quite good fun, I liked guessing at what they were like by looking at their faces and clothes and stuff. On my right was Mr X, late thirties, face partially hidden behind his daily newspaper. What I saw of his expression did little to persuade me that life was a bag of laughs for him. A deep frown he had, and small bags under his eyes. If I had to bet on what he was here for (which I would be doing if Bones was around), I'd say he had stomach ulcers due to a nagging wife and a baby that cried in the middle of the night. Poor bloke, I wouldn't exactly envy his position.

On my left beside Mr Miller was this youngish, quite attractive woman. Looked a bit like you, Karen, she was plumpish with a big arse (don't get annoyed). I'm afraid she was another who didn't exactly seem over the moon and her contribution to the negligible conversation in the place was nil. Now in this analysing game you've got to look for clues. For instance, this bird's plumpness might be because she was p-r-e-g-n-a-n-t. And judging by the morbid look on her face, the future newcomer to the world would be without a daddy, if you receive my drift.

This immature pastime soon got boring. So I decided, perhaps a little stupidly, to start talking to everyone.

'Well, isn't this nice?' I said confidently, tongue in cheek.

Everyone must have heard me and some people even (wait for it) looked up at me. But then they went back to reading their magazines pretty quickly. I suppose they weren't overjoyed at the sight of an unappealing adolescent shooting his mouth off. You'd have told me to shut up, for sure.

'You know, I've always said there's nowhere like a doctor's waiting room for meeting new people and having a good intellectual chat.'

No answer.

'I'm in here for Outer Mongolian flu, you know.' I hoped to shock people by saying that. It was the mischief in me. Still a child at heart, me.

'I didn't know you had Outer Mongolian flu, son.' Mr Miller sounded distraught.

'No. I was kidding,' I said, quieter.

'We had it at the front, you know. That flu stuff spread right through the ranks. Was worse in the trenches.'

'Mr Miller, will you go through now, please?' said the receptionist lady just as the old man was discussing flu in the First World War.

'That's me!' he exclaimed, pointing at himself.

'Yes.'

I helped him out of his seat. He moved slowly over to the doctor's room at the end of our waiting room. He was very, very stiff, Karen.

'Are you going to be all right, Mr Miller?' I asked.

'Aye, I'll survive.'

I believed him. I'd give him a terrific chance of living a long while yet because he's too stubborn to die.

Out of the doctor's room came Dr Lenart, the small chubby doctor. But I hardly noticed him. It was his patient that I saw.

'Righty-ho, Hannah, I'll see you again in two weeks,' he said jollily to this girl. It was her, Karen, the one that meant so much to me and yet I hardly knew. It was the first time I'd heard her name as well, and from then on every time I heard the name Hannah mentioned, no matter where or when, my mind transferred to her.

'Thank you, doctor.' She was dead polite. 'I'll see you.'

I was so amazed at seeing her, here of all places, that I didn't know what to do or say to her. My big chance and I was stuck for words. She came closer and did she look terrific? I don't mean OK terrific but crazy, out-of-this-world terrific. I was shaken by her presence. She wore one of those trendy dungaree suits, a purple colour it was. Underneath was a plain white T-shirt but there was nothing plain about her.

50

I must have looked a klutz, standing in the middle of a doctor's waiting room as she passed me by. She smiled at me though, Karen, so she must have remembered me from the supermarket. I'd never thought she'd actually remember me. I had to say something to her, I knew that. So I opened my mouth and hoped some words would come out.

'Hannah.'

She turned round, half wondering who'd said her name. But she was very relaxed.

'Have you got the time?'

OK so it's a corny thing to say, but like I say I had to say something.

'Have you got the energy?' she joked. She laughed and her face lit up. I tried to laugh too, but I was so bloody nervous that I'm not sure whether I did.

'It's quarter to six.'

I knew what the time was, of course. I'd been sitting opposite that boring old clock, you remember, for twenty minutes.

'Thank you,' I replied, trying desperately at the same time to think of something else to say to her. I tried to imagine that I was talking to a normal bird. If I could have spoken to her as I did to you, then it would have been much easier. As it was, she overwhelmed me. She almost scared me.

'Well. It's been nice talking to you,' she said. I reckon she was being sarcastic. A taste of my own medicine, huh?

'I've got to rush. I've got to catch a 59 bus. It's due now.'

'Sure.'

'I didn't catch your name,' she said, opening the exit door.

'Jason.'

'Jason,' she repeated. 'I'll see you around, Jason. You are the guy with the kid brother who destroyed the shop the other day.'

'That's me.'

She had remembered me. Te-ra.

And that was it. I felt so good, Karen, but if anything

51

she'd done the chatting up. Isn't the guy supposed to do all of that? Well, I didn't care, I was officially hooked on Hannah and I knew it.

SEVEN

Now discussing such matters as falling hopelessly for a bird is something I'm not used to at all. It's not the sort of thing a guy talks about to his mates, or to anyone else at that. But that doesn't mean the feelings weren't there inside of me.

I'll be honest with you, Karen, and I'll tell you that those feelings got the better of supposedly easy-going me. I had these urges to see her every day and I thought of her practically all the time. It sounds like the bull-shit stuff you read in your girly magazines, I know, but I suppose it happens to lads as well.

I got devious, and started using my brain in order to see her as much as possible without letting on I was stone crazy on her. She told me at the doctor's that she went on a 59 bus, right? So I got to thinking that, if I took that bus and all, I'd get to see her.

The first couple of times I took the 59 she wasn't on it. But I wasn't ready to be beaten so easily. I was willing to keep trying for years. I expect you're thinking, wouldn't it be hilarious if Jay did wait for years for Hannah and she never took the 59; but you're wrong because it was fourth time lucky (or was it fifth?).

And then I got to thinking about all the things you used to grab Simon's attention with. Yes, you told me all about the dropping of schoolbags in the corridor. If you could get away with corny numbers like that, then what I was doing was comparatively harmless.

That day, I needed time on my own. So I went to City Park and walked round in circles for an hour or two. It was a quiet place usually with perhaps a few tramps or people walking their dogs. The day I went there were no tramps or even people walking dogs. There was a group of nippers a few years older than Ed playing football with a battered leather football and jumpers as posts. I thought I'd be real smart and be the star of the game, which wouldn't have been totally amazing as I was sixteen and they were ten. So I asked whether I could play and they let me play only on the condition I paid the match-fee of 10p. Right bunch of sods they were, Karen. So I'm playing this game of football and I get the ball in my own half. I do my Georgie Best skills taking it round first one, then two and another. The goal's in sight and I have a massive whack hoping to score goal of the month but I fall right on my backside. You know when sometimes you fall over and take it in good humour. Well it wasn't like that because I had a great line of mud on the seat of my trousers. And besides I felt a right fool.

'You're not all that good at all, are you?' said one of these little hooligans.

'How'd you like your face rubbed in the mud?'

'You're not playing.'

I got up slowly and limped away. It was raining, Karen, and it was dark enough for the street-lamps to be on. The water from the tree-lined pavements by the park dripped on to me and the grassy bits were stodgy with the sponged up mud. In my misery, I glanced at my watch. It was five to five. The 59 went on the hour and I'd no intention of missing it. I ran like the wind, Karen, as fast as I could. My jogging had come in handy after all. It was wet and uncomfortable running through the park but I only thought of getting to that bus stop.

Breathless, I arrived at the bus shelter where there was a queue of people. I asked the woman beside me whether the 59 had gone.

'Oh ... I'm not sure, dear. Yes, I think it has.'

'Shit.' I think it came out a bit loud because I got some nasty looks from those in the queue. I thought one old dear beside me was going to hit me with her handbag. I do make

54

efforts to cut down on swearing and I never swear in front of Mum. I was just frustrated that day; well, how would you feel?

Beside the woman I'd asked the time was a real cute little girl sucking her thumb. I seemed to be surrounded by nippers. What with Ed and those lads that I played football with. Not that I minded youngsters, they're more relaxing to be with, you don't feel a need to impress them. This little girl spoke to her mum on hearing me swear.

'Mummy, that man said a rude word.'

'Yes, and he's very naughty.'

'Does that mean Daddy's naughty when he says it as well?' That knocked her mum back.

'Now don't be silly, Jenny. Daddy doesn't swear because he knows it's wrong.'

'Does so.'

'No, he doesn't.'

'What about that time he hit that nail into his finger with the hammer?'

'Be quiet!'

I sniggered, the woman didn't look very pleased with me.

'Here comes your bus,' she remarked sternly.

'Oh.'

I hadn't missed it after all. Wow, I was happy at that, I had that feeling that after all this she was bound to be on it today. Call it your brother's psychic ability. I wasn't wrong.

As I went to order my ticket I saw her sitting on the fourth from front seat on the left hand side. It's difficult to describe exactly how I felt. I don't think there's a great need to explain that unexplainable feeling to you. It has to be the same excitement and thrill you had with Simon. Can I take this moment to apologise for my teasing of you after your marshmallowy stories of 'melting in Simon's arms'?

'Yes, sir?' the bus driver looked at me.

'Pardon.'

'What do you want?'

'Uh?'

'Where do you want to go?' he said, getting impatient. I

was in a daze at seeing Hannah. Hell, Karen, I didn't know what I was saying.

'I don't rightly know where to go.'

'We've got a case here,' the driver said to the people waiting to order their tickets. 'Look, sir, we go to a number of places on this route. I'll be here till next year if I tell you all of them.'

I wasn't listening to him, I looked at Hannah. She saw me and smiled.

'I'm waiting, sir.'

'Oh, I'll go anywhere, any place will do.'

'Been drinking this afternoon?'

'No.'

'Well, you're not making sense. I'll give you a 25p ticket to Alton Road because there's a doctor there and you need one.'

'Cheers. How much will that be?'

He sighed.

'Well, for a 25p bus ticket, I'll charge you twenty-five new pennies, just for a novelty.'

I smiled and gave him the exact money, told him to keep the change and started to walk towards Hannah, only to be called back because I'd forgotten to take my ticket.

What a jerk I am, Karen. I wouldn't have minded, if Hannah hadn't seen it all. The seat where she sat had a space beside it. I got to ask her for that seat. That's pretty brave, isn't it? I was terrified she'd say no, but she was really pleasant about it.

'Yeah, of course.' She smiled glowingly.

I sat down and tried to calm my nerves.

'You were a long time buying your ticket,' she said.

'The driver wasn't quite with it,' I lied. No doubt I blushed.

'I see.' She smiled reassuringly. 'You don't normally come on this bus, do you? I haven't seen you before.'

'No, I'm not usually on here actually, well not at all really. I missed my usual bus and took this not so usual bus so I wouldn't have to wait for another usual bus.'

You couldn't wish to hear more verbal diarrhoea than that. I was so nervous, though. By that time I was sure she'd written me off as a complete case, but would you believe she nodded as if she actually understood what I was saying; like she was helping me along. You know as well as me that loads of birds wouldn't have made it so easy.

'We seem to be seeing each other all over the place.'

'Yeah, it's funny.'

'I noticed the uniform. You're from Cartland, aren't you?'

'Afraid so. I'm not over-keen on it, I'm afraid.'

'Yeah, my best friend goes there and she isn't enjoying it very much either.'

'Which friend is that?'

'Lucy Norton,' she said, answering my question.

'Oh yes, I know her quite well. She's in one of my classes.'

I hardly knew her at all. She lived down Malton Terrace, went to my playgroup when we were little kids. I forget, but didn't she have a brother your age? I wasn't wild about the girl now, but I realised she must have something going for her if she knew Hannah.

'She was going out with Michael Leonard,' I added, to show that I knew her quite well.

'She chucked him.'

'Oh dear,' I said, all wet.

'It doesn't matter. He was a right hunk. He wasn't natural enough, I prefer natural boys.'

At which point I tried extremely hard to act all natural. Come on, Karen, what is a bird's exact definition of 'natural'? Don't tell me, 'Simon was natural'.

'This is my stop,' she said politely as we approached Elliot Road, 'So would you excuse me?'

'Sure.'

I got up like a real gentleman and she went past me. I saw her up real close and she meant everything to me, Karen. I loved her. You know the bus did drop me off near the doctor's surgery and I walked four miles home and I didn't mind one bit.

EIGHT

Things really started moving for me then, Karen. This is the best part of my story, I began not to care what anyone thought of me because only one person mattered. You know, I even had the guts to tell Lenny Burton to stick his dope us his arse when he asked me whether I wanted to buy any. How about that? And in front of Carl and Justin.

Thinking about it, my school and social life practically collapsed around me at that time. I got chucked out of the football team because I'd missed all but one training session. Well, I blame it on a personality clash between me and the manager. (You called it that, so I'm saying it as well). I guess my schoolwork didn't exactly prosper during that period. I put that one down to my concentration level, which had been emotionally disturbed. Sounds good, doesn't it?

Another event which happened at that time which was in the end to leave an impression on me was to do with Cookie. Poor Cookie, his bird chucked him after a week and four days and not only was Cookie shattered, but I lost my bet with Bones.

He told me about it on this trip to London we went on. It was one of these day trips with the school which is meant to be intellectually stimulating, but which is a good doss in reality. OK, I know we had to see a play in the afternoon, but we had the whole morning to do what we wanted.

Guess where Justin, Bones and Andy Markham went? St. Paul's? No. Buckingham Palace? The Tate Gallery? No, Karen, they went to Soho. To be honest (which I'm being yet again) I'd have gone too, but Cookie was on his own and wanted to go to see Arsenal's football ground. And being the super-nice guy that you know I am, I felt sorry for him and offered to tour with him.

It was while we were looking for this never-to-be-found football ground that he brought out all his troubles and bad news. He hadn't told anyone before me that she'd ditched him, because it had only happened the previous day. This was heavy stuff, Karen. He was trusting me like none of my other mates had ever done. I suppose he hadn't got an older sister. Yeah, they do have their advantages. Not that mine's been around lately.

'She chucked me,' he complained, quite out of the blue whilst we were walking in a busy London street with loads of people around.

'Uh?'

'She left me. One minute we're together and the next...'

'Why?'

'I don't know. We'd only been together a few times and I felt loads of tension.'

'I'm not with you,' I said, which was a pretty unhelpful thing to say.

'She told me that we weren't getting on. At first I thought she liked me but as time went on I got these feelings that she'd gone off me. When we went out I was nervous with her, even to put my arm around her. And I even began stuttering a bit and I haven't done that for years.'

'Nerves, Cookie.'

'Yes.' He looked empty; his eyes were hidden behind his glasses.

'You kiss her?' I asked, looking at him.

'Well, sort of.'

I laughed.

'Cookie, either you kiss or you don't.' It was a pretty unsympathetic thing to say. It wasn't meant that way, Karen.

'Oh, forget it,' he said.

That made me feel lousy. I stopped dead in the street.

'No, I'm sorry. I was only kidding. I want to hear about it.'

'Look, it's not your problem.'

He walked away. Really choked up he was. I'd never seen him like that, not even after the lads had given him stick. He always seemed capable of handling it.

'Cookie,' I followed him, 'tell me about it.'

'OK.' He tried to look happier. 'Jay, we're not going to find this crap football ground, so let's go and have a coffee somewhere. It's on me.'

We went to a quiet seedy little place on the corner of a street. Run down this cafe was, but the coffee was only 17p a cup.

Cookie told me all there was to tell in there.

'I sort of kissed her . . . but I pulled myself back because I felt she wouldn't want to know, like I thought she was going to reject me. Well, look at me, Jay, what am I? A seventeen-year-old mug with glasses who stutters when he gets real nervous.'

'You seem OK.'

'Jay, I'm not stupid.'

I felt uncomfortable. 'Look, we're not all Robert Redfords, you know. Or even Lenny Burtons.'

We both laughed, he for the first time. In fact he thought that so funny that he nearly spat his coffee all over the cafe. I was pleased that he could smile at something, he seemed so sad. He had no confidence at all, and in a world where the 'morons' were cocky and self-satisfied, he didn't have the cynicism or roughness to keep up.

'I don't know, Jay,' he continued, talking freely now, 'I'm not far off eighteen and my experience with birds is two disastrous cock-ups. Every time I go out with a girl everyone sees it as a joke and has bets on how long it will last.'

'I'm sorry about th. . .'

'It doesn't matter, Jay,' he smiled. 'I don't blame anyone except myself. If only me and her could have hit it off.'

'Don't over-rate her,' I said.

'I know. She's going out with another boy already. Richard Thail. I heard about it just this morning. How could she go out with a twat like him?' he despaired.

I agreed.

'There we go again,' he added. 'Laughing at other people again. All we ever do, when we're not handing it out to each other we'll give stick to other people.'

'That's the way it goes,' I said, trying to be philosophical. Don't laugh, Karen – I can be philosophical when I try.

'Hey, Cooks, it's not far off 12.00, we'd better be on our way.'

'Oh crap, that boring play.'

'I'm bound to fall asleep. I always do.'

'Yeah, and we've wasted a morning. I told my Dad I was going to one of the museums, and we end up in a cafe.'

'Well, it's not been totally wasted,' I sighed, leaving my empty coffee cup on the table.

'No, it hasn't. Thanks for listening, Jay. I didn't mean to go on.'

When Cookie said that you had the feeling he meant it. On your own with Cookie, you got to do a lot of straight talking, it made a change.

We met up at the theatre. Quite a modern place it was, real plush with bars and shops at the back. Too nice for our lot. Justin and Bones were really going on about what a terrific morning they'd had in Soho. What a bunch of jokers.

'You should have seen the place, Jay. All porno shops and flicks. A real laugh.'

'Yeah, and then we went into this topless bar,' said Bones. No, Karen, I didn't believe him either.

'Oh good; and Cookie and me saw a flying saucer in Hyde Park. You talk some crap.'

'Honest, it was a doddle, man. We couldn't believe how easy it was, just strolled into this sleazy joint and ordered a drink. And they had these birds, you should have seen it.' Justin was practically frothing at the mouth with excitement.

We began to walk into the actual theatre bit. Our seats

61

were near the back, which was good because we could fall asleep without the actors and actresses noticing.

'You're all mouth, Justin,' I sneered.

'Better than going to some football ground in the middle of nowhere.'

'Didn't go there.'

'Where d'you go then?'

'Tower of London. It was ace.'

'Well, there was no way it could match Soho. Bones bought this sex potion stuff.'

I looked at Cookie and he looked at me.

'Sex what?' said Cookie.

'Sex potion, me and Andy each bought a bottle off this bloke. It had a real unpronounceable name but what it really meant was that it was the body perfumes that make a bird fancy a guy.'

Bones pulled out this minute bottle, smaller than a perfume bottle. I had a look at it and smelt it. It had no smell.

'It's got no odour.'

Cookie smelt it as well and said, 'He's right, it's got no smell.'

'It's not supposed to, you twats. It has a subconscious effect on birds. And the bloke I bought it off said it had been scientifically proved that guys who wear it have a 70% better chance of pulling the birds.'

I kept silent for a second, trying to keep myself from laughing at Bones who'd obviously been taken. Then I broke down. Ah, Karen, who'd be dumb enough to go for that? Don't answer that.

'You've been conned,' I said.

'Like shit I have.'

'OK, Bones. If that bottled stuff is sex potion and not water then prove it. See that girl with the hazel hair two rows down sitting on her own. Put some of that stuff on and try it out with her.'

I was only kidding. But he took it dead serious.

'You're on,' he said, and proceeded to chuck this stuff all

over his neck, rubbing it into his skin. We couldn't believe it when he went ahead and started to chat up this lone girl who was much too classy for him. You can imagine it, Karen, it was such a laugh. But he'd really been suckered by this con man. He sincerely believed the stuff worked.

Well, he went right close to this classy girl hoping she'd mysteriously fall for him; we watched from our seats eager to see the outcome. He said something to her. I couldn't make out exactly what he said, but it didn't matter because in a second he was making his way back up to us, shaking his head in disbelief.

'She told me to go away,' he said sadly. 'I felt a right jerk.'

'You looked one,' I laughed hysterically. 'That proves the stuff's a fake.'

'But I don't understand it. The bloke said it worked without fail.'

'The bloke was a crook.'

'No chance, he said it had a 70% success rate, I must have been in the unlucky thirty.'

'Sure, Bones, sure,' I said, still laughing.

It was a riot, Karen. I was still chuckling when the lights faded and the play began. As for the play, it was so boring I nearly died. I can't even recall the title, you'd have probably adored it. In the end, I fell asleep during the third act.

NINE

It was soon after that day in London that Justin had his big
moment in life. He got his 50 c.c. motorbike and it became
his one and only love. After that day all he'd talk about was
how the clutch had gone or that he was going to respray it in
yellow. As if it mattered. He was the first of our group to get
a bike; since then Bones has got one. Marshall said he's
waiting until his eighteenth birthday before he gets a bike
and as for Carl, well, he hasn't mastered a push-bike yet so
a motorcycle's way beyond him.

Of course, bikes never thrilled me. It was you who always
wanted one, not that Mum was ever going to let a delicate
lady risk her neck on a Kawasaki. And after all that,
Richard D. Ives drives his car and you into a tree.

Justin really thought he had one over us the day he got
that bike. He thought he was some sort of star with his fancy
hairstyle and his 50 c.c. job. Because we knew he'd be so
cocky, we all decided to pretend we hadn't noticed his new
bike even though we had. Pretty mean, huh, Karen?

So poor Justin brought it over for us to see that Thursday
lunchtime thinking we'd be impressed and all. He dragged
us all outside to take a look and proudly showed it off.

'Look at that!' He stood in front of it as if he was expecting
someone to take a photo of him. We all pretended not to
notice the bike in front of us. There must have been four or
five of us.

'Yeah,' said Carl, all uninterested.

The rest of us nodded drearily.

'Got it today,' he continued. 'Looks a gem, don't it? I've
tried it out this morning.'

'It's all right,' I said.

'Well, why don't you all come and have a proper look at it? Come on, get closer.'

'Oh no thanks, Justin. It's a bit cold out here. I'm going in.'

'My good friend,' said Lenny, 'I've got better things to do.'

We all started walking in, pretending not to care about the bike.

'Well, that's real enthusiasm, lads,' shouted Justin as we went off. 'The next time any of you have got anything new to show off don't come to me. I won't take a bit of notice.'

'Hey Justin,' called Carl, 'you know who you remind me of?'

'No.'

'The Fonz.'

We all laughed.

'Up yours, Carl,' said Justin, by now getting his knickers in a twist.

'Hey-y-y-y-y,' Carl added, doing perhaps the worst imitation of the Fonz that I'll ever be privileged to hear. Yes, Karen, his imitations were worse than mine of Tommy Cooper and Bruce Forsyth.

The school inside was much warmer than outside. We stood by this heater thing which blew out warm air. It was in the main hall area; there was hardly anyone there at lunchtimes apart from the odd kid.

'He's wasting his money on that bike,' said one lad.

'Yeah,' Lenny added, 'there are loads of other things to spend money on. Concerts, booze, dope, birds. Mind you, lads, a bit of advice. Be careful what you spend on them. I took some lass out to that fair in the summer and I spent about three quid on her. And at the end of the evening she said thank you and went home. Not even a kiss, I got nothing out of her.'

Not like Lenny, I thought.

'Was she tight?' said Carl.

'Too right, she was.'

'Who was the girl, Lenny?'

'Oh I don't know. It was a blind date . . . Hannah she was called. One of Lucy Norton's friends.'

And then the penny dropped and I realised he was talking about the one and only Hannah. And for the first time I felt all insecure about how I might lose her without having her.

'I chucked her the next day. Won't see her again,' Lenny carried on. I was kind of relieved he didn't like her because although he was talking about her like she was muck, at the same time I didn't want to compete for her with anybody, let alone a stud like Lenny.

All this talk got me so panicky and worried that I decided to see her immediately. It had to be that lunchtime, Karen. I was out of the school in a second, still all hyped up and crazy inside. When I arrived at the supermarket the girl at the delicatessen told me she'd gone to the park for her lunch-break.

Now City Park is a big place when you're looking for one person and I thought I might miss her. But as I went towards the playground area I saw her from quite a distance. She was sitting on a bench eating her lunch and watching the kids on the swings. She had a beige-coloured coat on and her hair was blowing in the wind. All alone she was, Karen, I couldn't work out why she was on her own so much. In my more ridiculous moments I thought it was destiny that she was on her own whenever I saw her, like an opportunity for me to talk to her on a one to one. You can laugh, Karen, but you've been through this yourself. Just think back a year or so.

I walked tentatively towards her, checking that I was looking reasonable. I felt flustered.

'Hullo,' I said as I sat down on the bench beside her.

'Hi. I'm sorry that I'm talking with my mouth full, but this is my lunch.'

She was real polite.

'Oh, don't worry.'

'It's my mum's sandwiches. Would you like one?'

'Oh, no thanks, I'm not hungry.'

'They're nice. Not poisoned or anything.'

She smiled, I noticed it when she smiled.

'I'm sure they're delicious. But I've eaten at school and that's quite enough.'

'Are you enjoying school?' she asked.

'I get by,' that was my standard answer whenever I was asked about school. 'I may have made a mistake going into the sixth-form, I should have gone straight into a job.'

'My parents said I should have stayed on, but I didn't care for it. I like my work.'

'Sounds fair enough.'

'And teachers didn't get on with me.'

'Oh, I don't believe it,' I said jokingly. She laughed. She was relaxed, Karen, she was at ease and gave the impression that she didn't know the meaning of the word nervous.

I changed the subject.

'I hear you went out with Lenny Burton.'

'Oh, yuk!' She pulled a face. 'I keep it quiet. You know he took me to the fair and every ride we went on he tried to get his feelers all over me.'

'Sounds like Lenny.'

'Did he say anything about me?'

'Not much.'

'I should think he said I'm tight.'

'No . . . he said you didn't get along, something like that.' She sneered.

'So you don't like him?' I had to know for definite.

'No chance.'

'Good.'

I know I should have asked her out then, but I held back. You birds don't make it any easier either. It's always us who have to put our lives on the line by asking for the date. And more often than not, you'll make us seem small by refusing and giving some absurd excuse. I wanted to tell her what I thought of her, Karen, like Simon was able to tell you, but I chickened out. I regret it now.

'It's a horrible day,' she said.

'Yeah, dead windy.'

'I hate days like this, don't you?'

'Oh yes, they're lousy.'

She'd finished her sandwiches and put her waste paper in the bin.

'I've got to hop off now. If I'm not back at the shop soon my boss will give me the sack.'

'I won't keep you.'

Away she went, waving to me as she disappeared from the park. I waved back and stayed sat on the same bench for half an hour, thinking. I didn't notice the cold.

Ed and me went to Jill's house one Sunday. It was the Sunday after I'd seen Hannah because I had her on my mind all the way to Grantham and Dad kept asking me why I was so quiet. They thought I was scared of meeting Jill's family, but that didn't bother me at all.

You never did meet her family, did you, Karen? Shame. I can tell you that they were a right bunch of odd-balls. I'm not sure why she lived with her parents anyway. You probably did the right thing, getting out when you did. Not that I thank you for it.

It was a real posh house on the outskirts of Grantham. They must have been loaded. It was the sort of place where it took you half an hour to get up the drive. The actual house was more like a mansion, black and white timber it was, like Newcastle United's football kit. Ed thought it *was* another castle! Inside, it looked like a palace, all antiques and sherry decanters and framed pictures.

We had Sunday afternoon tea out on the lawn which looked like a bowling green. There were four people in Jill's family counting herself. Mr and Mrs were your normal rich couple. Both in the mid fifties, he was a retired businessman with enough money to supply sufficient food to fill his gusset belly. He looked a bit like Winston Churchill except he didn't wear a suit. She was the loving housewife, amateur cook and croquet player, very upper class.

'One lump or two, Jeremy?' (She always called me Jeremy.)

'Three, please.'

'Oh, I say,' she said, all shocked as if I'd pulled my trousers down in front of her. 'You are a sweet tooth. I expect you'd like a piece of cherry cake that I've made.'

I hated cherry cake. All those red lumps in a stodgy mess. Yuk, it was worse than your fruit cake, which is saying something.

'It looks delicious,' I said.

'Mother's a keen cook,' said Jill, eager to keep the conversation going.

'Oh, I do enjoy it,' she said. 'Jill's father does like his food. So I try to make some tasty recipes.'

'She does make a good cherry cake,' claimed Mr Jill, slumped in his deckchair, and munching his food down.

'Mum, tell them about the contest.'

'Oh, no, we hear this story every time. Bores me to tears,' groaned Mr Jill.

'I'd like to hear it,' said Dad, all humble. He was creeping up to Jill's parents, I could tell. Not that I blame him, Karen, it was just so obvious.

'Well, it was all very exciting. I entered the *Woman's Own* do-it-yourself cookery contest for 1979. I didn't think I had a hope of winning.'

'What did you cook?' said Dad, slowly sipping his tea.

'For starters I carved out some hard boiled egg whites and garnished them with a sprinkling of parsley and grated cheese and covered them with a lavish helping of mayonnaise. Then for the main course I decided to make Porc au Vin, a French dish which involves cooking pork in a wine sauce and covering it with breadcrumbs. I thought it would be best to serve the meat with diced carrots and green beans because . . .'

She wouldn't stop. I couldn't believe what a bore it was listening to someone who'd entered a cooking contest. Dad and Jill pretended it was the most fascinating thing they'd heard since man walked on the moon. But Mr Jill yawned out loud and Ed, not surprisingly, got all restless. He started running in circles around the dainty tea table. I was terrified he was going to knock it over. It would have been so typical wouldn't it, Karen?

Then we were graced by the appearance of the fourth member of the family, Jill's brother Colin. A youth of twenty with incredibly tight-fitting blue jeans and a T-shirt saying 'I'm a virgin – this shirt was made 10 years ago'. Another stud, I thought.

At least he interrupted the conversation. Jill did the introductions.

'Jason and Edward, I'd like you to meet my brother Colin.'

'Hey, Jason, how you doing?'

'Terrific, and you?'

'Fine, and you Edward?' He tapped Ed on the head. The wee man looked bemused.

'Hey man, how would you like to look around the old house, then? I've got a fine stereo system in my room.'

'Colin is a disc-jockey. Spends his life playing over-rated music for half-witted kids,' said the old man.

'Now now, Arnold, don't insult the boy.'

'Sorry, dear.'

Colin was too dumb to be upset by his Dad's insults and he merrily gave us a tour of his house. Not to be missed, this, Karen.

'Hey, Jay. You can call me Zeb.'

'I thought you were called Colin.'

'My parents call me Colin, but Zeb sounds so much better.'

'OK, Zeb it is.'

He showed Ed and me his room. It was a fine room, to do him justice. He had it all in order with a good record player and tape deck. Also on one side of the room he had a massive collection of model soldiers, all individually painted. Ed was loving it.

'Soldiers!' he exclaimed and he rushed over to the table and started fiddling with them.

'Hey, Ed. Don't mess with them, please,' Zeb said strongly.

'It's a good collection, Zeb.'

'Yeah, I've got two hundred and seventy regiments. At this very moment I'm playing out the Anglo-Prussian War. It's a fine hobby to have. I'm really into it.'

Now don't forget this guy's twenty years, not twenty months.

'You got a wench?' he said, changing the subject and catching me by surprise.

'Um ... not as such.'

'Ah well, at sixteen you tend to be feeling your way. All sex at your age; sex and puppy love.'

'I don't know about ...'

'When I was sixteen I was a right little sod. I haven't met a single sixteen-year-old who wasn't after only one thing with a girl. I first screwed a bird at sixteen, you know, right tart she was, she said she was seventeen but I reckon she was under age.'

Another kid telling me his life story. He made me want to puke all over his model soldiers, all two hundred and seventy regiments of them. He was the sort of stud that you feminists would want to put up against a wall and shoot. Certainly you'd have gone into that speech you gave me from time to time, about male chauvinist pigs and women as sex objects. Yeah, you were destined to be a liberated woman with a good career and all that. What I couldn't figure out was after all this 'I don't need men' talk, you'd go out with Richard D. Ives. Now Simon I can understand, but Richard D. Ives? Who in his right mind puts the middle letter in his name? I'd be called a pratt if I wrote on my essays, Jason L. Border. I thought that kid would be no good, Karen. You told me there'd be no one like Simon ever again, and you were right.

I'm sorry, Karen, this has nothing to do with Zeb. He gave me all this blab about sixteen-year-olds being after one thing. I wouldn't have touched Hannah, if she hadn't wanted me to. Being with her would have been enough.

That's not soppy or prudish or stupid, it's how one sixteen-year-old feels.

On the way back from Grantham I told Dad what a tough time he'd have putting up with Zeb and Mr and Mrs Jill. He didn't mind them, though; told me to be more tolerant. Typical of him, people didn't bug him. If a friend did something wrong, he'd let it pass over his head and concentrate on the things the friend did right. I couldn't do that. I used to be able to switch off like that, but like I said, I changed.

TEN

Now, Karen, Lucy Norton (whose claim to fame was being Hannah's best friend) was to play an important part in this cosy little story. Becoming more devious by the day, I worked out a plan to get in with Hannah. By talking with Lucy I might manage to get closer to her. I felt sort of guilty because I was using Lucy, but then loads of kids do it. It's the classic manoeuvre used by creeps to get on the right side of someone they fancy. You think back to all the boys in your class who very coincidentally got to know me well. Naively I used to ask, 'why does that Ken David always come round our house?' Wow, was I thick.

Now in order to see Lucy more, I paid the price. And that price was heavy; Art Appreciation Society. No, I'm not joking, Karen. I spent hours at the A.A.S., lunch-hours at that, analysing paintings and sculpture. All in the cause of one girl. Really bad, huh, I felt a right jerk but it had to be done.

Lucy was quite nice as it turned out. Your average, mature, hard-working girl with long legs, pleasant smile and tidy hairstyle. Some lads hammered her because they thought she had a slight squint. I didn't notice it, so what if she did have a squint?

She (like everyone else) showed genuine surprise when I first walked into that art class on Monday lunchtime. Her mouth dropped open like a fish when she saw me. My embarrassment wasn't eased by the squeals of laughter from the girlies who were taken aback at seeing this dosser in their class. 'What's Jason Border doing here? Oh, he doesn't seem like an intellectual. Lardy dah – how intriguing.' No one exactly came up to see me and asked me what the hell I was doing in the A.A.S. but I could see the looks on their smug faces. And you can stop laughing yourself, Karen.

It was all very difficult. What would the lads say? I tried to keep it secret from them, of course, but they were bound to find out. Ah well, I thought to myself. Maybe Carl, Bones and company would understand and realise that people's interests at Sixth Form were diverse. Sure, they'd be totally reasonable about the whole incident ...

'You big puff!' Carl mocked as I strolled out of the first Monday lunchtime meeting.

'I see you heard, lads.'

'We heard it from Bones. Since when have you become an art fanatic, Jay?' said Marshall.

'Oh, I've liked art for quite a while.'

Justin was disgusted; he was the sort of kid who'd take World War III in his stride yet would go crazy mad if you lost his pencil.

'Jay, you're running closely for the pratt of the year award, along with Cookie and Walter Todd.'

'Cookie's all right.'

'Sticking up for Cookie now; another change in your personality,' noted Carl.

'No.'

There I was, backing off again when challenged. Of course I was sticking up for Cookie, which was good, wasn't it? Yet Carl made it seem like a crime, so I backed off into my shell. Like always, except now I at least was feeling guilty every time I took it out of Cookie. I'd hardly felt guilty before, which is good in a way. With no guilt you're free to do what you want, nothing's stopping you. That's how I've changed since you last saw me. I wanted you to know that.

'I reckon Cookie's a bit of a pratt because of his roots. They're mad,' said Marshall who didn't seem to be over troubled with guilt himself. 'You didn't see the other night, Jay. We were coming home from the pub and out of nowhere Cookie's old man pulls up in his Ferrari and tells Cookie to get in.'

74

'And?'

'And then he tells Cookie that he hasn't done his chores. I'd be hating it if I were Cookie, I'd tell my roots to get stuffed.'

'I'm sure they'd appreciate that.'

'I'm a survivor, I'll tell you that,' Marshall said. That hit the nail on the head.

This A.A.S. lark was too much, Karen. It had to end, so I got to talk to Lucy after one of the sessions. She was with her friends when I approached her. They reminded me of you. Either they talked about matters of great intellectual significance, or ridiculously petty, girly mush about the colour of their new lipsticks.

I'd already planned what to say to Lucy.

'Excuse me.'

'Yes,' she replied, half looking around to see if I might be talking to someone else.

'Would it be possible to borrow your book on Artistic Perspectives?'

She was carrying this big blue book with a picture of Da Vinci on it. I didn't really want it but it was a way of making conversation. She was suspicious of me, I could tell.

'Of course you can ... if you truly want to.'

'Oh, I truly do.'

She passed the book over to me and I lobbed it in my school-bag.

'Funny, I don't envisage you as an artistic person.'

'Ah-ha, appearances can be deceptive.'

'True.' She looked at me doubtfully. 'Yes ... why not?'

'There is one other thing. To do with Hannah ...'

'Oh, so that's what all this is about. Yes, I've heard of you two love-birds. She keeps telling me about you, to tell you the truth she bores me to tears when she goes on about you. You asked her out yet?'

'No.'

'Chicken.'

'I know, that's why I was ...'

'Hoping I'd do your dirty work. I tell you what, Jason.

You know Al's disco, meet her there at 8.30. She likes dancing.'

'I can't dance.'

'Start practising, deary, because she thinks you can walk on water.'

'No.'

'Oh yes, Jason. God knows why.' She winked at me, I laughed. It was incredible, Karen, she actually fancied me. I thought I'd have to work at that bit.

'Thanks, Lucy.'

'Don't thank me . . . Oh Jason, you won't be needing that book.'

'No, I wasn't going to read it.'

'You couldn't fool me. Appearances can be deceptive, what a load of rubbish. I can see through you like I can see through that window,' she boasted.

And sure enough, I quit the A.A.S. that minute, never to grace its meetings again. I doubt whether they missed me, Karen.

Lucy walked up to me on the Wednesday while I was talking to the lads. She only said two words, but they were pretty important – 'It's on'. That's all she said, leaving me with a wry smile on my face and the lads totally bemused. Of course they wanted to know what was going on. But I wouldn't let it slip, it really annoys people when there's a secret you have which you won't tell them. The lads were racking their brains out. 'Surely you're not going with her?' 'No.' 'Is there some party on?' 'No.' Justin threatened to duff me in if I didn't tell them, but that only succeeded in making me laugh.

So, what were you doing on Friday October 25th, Karen? What do you mean, you don't remember? I thought this was going to be the biggest day of my life. From that year on, I figured it would become a national holiday (don't take that too seriously).

To forget about it, I went boozing on Wednesday and

Thursday. It was on the Thursday that I let my well kept secret out. The lads were talking casually about things. Oh, I think Marshall was moaning about his lack of money. He blamed it on his mum. Poor woman, huh?

'Well,' I announced, 'I'm going to need some money for tomorrow night.'

'Not a shit A.A.S. meeting,' Carl jeered. 'Hey everyone, Rembrandt's got a meeting.' Rembrandt was my nickname now, due to my artistic connections.

'Swallow this one, Carl. I'm going to a ... a disco.'

Naturally, this caused an uproar. Don't forget the rules, Karen. No discos allowed. I had to explain why I was going.

'Look, I'm meeting a girl there, you don't think I'd go to a disco if I didn't have an excuse.'

'You meeting a girl at the disco?' said Marshall, all interested at the mention of a bird.

'Yeah, Marshall, I thought I'd try going out with a bird to a disco, I'm getting bored with boys, ducky.'

'Who is she?' he asked undeterred.

'Not telling you.'

'Does she go to Cartland?'

The questions came far and wide. Everyone except Cookie was eager to know who it was. He sat there on his stool, just outside the main circle, sipping his beer slowly and looking blank.

I ignored the questions.

'Hey, I could do with a game of pool. I feel in good form today ...'

'Rembrandt, you've never played a good game of pool in your life,' said Carl, so nicely. 'Now tell us about her.'

'Yeah, Jay.'

'All right, all right. If it will keep you quiet. She's a friend of Lucy Norton's. That's what she was telling me about yesterday.'

'I bet she's horrible,' Marshall said jealously.

'Richter scale – mark 10.1.'

'You can't go that high.'

'You haven't seen this girl.' That was about as close as I

got to actually telling them how much she meant to me.

'Tits,' said Justin, all out of the blue.

I laughed.

'Yeah, she's got a couple of those.'

'You know what I mean. Are they big? What size?'

'I'm afraid I haven't got the exact measurements. I'll give you an approximation after I've had a closer look.'

I felt myself showing off, but I didn't stop. I sounded like all the other lads, saying all the cocky things that I hate and despise when I hear other people saying them. You'd have been ashamed of me, Karen. I was ashamed of myself, afterwards.

'You fancy your chances?' Carl smiled.

I put my thumbs up.

'How long till you get your end away?'

'Maybe soon, if I'm lucky.'

Oh Karen, I didn't believe what I said. For one thing I made Hannah sound cheap, which was one thing she wasn't. Also made me sound like a stud, which I wasn't. And most of all, Hannah really was special; but how could I tell them that without them laughing at me for being soppy?

'I'm off,' said a voice from the background. 'I've got some work to do.' It was Cookie. No one said anything except me.

'I'll come too, Cooks. You coming, Justin?'

'No, you go on, Rembrandt.'

I finished my beer and stumbled out of the pub with Cookie. I felt a bit dizzy, I think it was because of the stuffiness of the place more than the beer. When we got outside, the freshness hit me like oxygen. The air was cold and gave me new vigour. Even so we didn't say much as we'd both had a fair amount to drink. You know what I was like after a drop or two. It made me say stupid things.

'I feel dizzy,' he said. He looked it too, Karen.

'Me and all.'

'You know what I like about drinking a lot, Jay . . . I may slur my words but I never stutter. Isn't that good?'

'Terrific.'

'So you've got yourself a girl. I hope you have more luck

with her than me. You can't do worse.' It was a pathetic comment, Karen.

'I'm a bit nervous about the disco.' I did my imitation of a fifth rate John Travolta on the pavement. 'I can't dance, but I'll try anything for her.'

'She's nice, is she?'

'Oh yeah. Special ... Cookie, you know that stuff I was saying about screwing her and all the wise talk, that's all it was, wise talk.' It was safe to tell Cookie. He was like you, I knew he wouldn't laugh. 'Hey, maybe you'd like to come to the disco with me. You could suss out some birds.'

'Hold it, Jay. I've done enough sussing out of birds.' He half tripped over a paving stone, I'd never seen him so strange as this before. Not drunk, but acting weird. 'My parents wouldn't like me to go to a disco. A waste of time, they'll say. Do your chores ...' he mumbled away.

'Tell 'em to boil their heads,' I said over-exuberantly. And I hammered you, for overreacting! Put that one down to the beer, Karen.

'I don't think I'll do that.' He laughed, again in a weird way as if he thought it wasn't funny.

'You OK?'

'Yeah, I got a headache. I'll make it.'

We parted ways at the corner of the High Street and the road leading to the bus station. I watched him for two hundred yards as he left me. I knew there was something wrong, Karen, it was that feeling I had. But I left him and forgot about it.

ELEVEN

Friday night did arrive. So did Mum at 6.20.

'Fish and chips tonight, boys,' she said as she entered. Her hands were full with grub and handbags and packages. She looked totally drained and whacked, she always was on Friday evenings. Us kids often took over at the weekend. She's always so tired, Karen.

'Is Edward here?'

Her slightly worried question was answered by Edward rushing into her like a miniature double-decker bus with no brakes. The result was a pile of fish and chips on the floor.

'You little sod, you've done it again,' I sighed, picking the stuff off the now not so clean floor.

'Don't swear at Edward, please, Jason. He's only six.'

'You wait until you hear what he's done to Tasha's birthday cake. Mrs Denby got it out to show him, so what do you think he did? Stuck his finger right in the middle of it and made a stonking hole in it.'

Yeah, he really did that. I never did like Mrs Denby! And then the kid started crying. Sure enough, it made me feel all bad about how mean I'd been. So I tried making it up.

'Come on, wee man, I'll put the chips on the table and you get the bread out.'

'And the butter.'

'And the butter.'

He galloped into the kitchen. He loved getting out the bread and butter. He wants to be a waiter now, that's after watching an excerpt about restaurants on Play School. I think he's ruled out the police, though he reckons he'd join the army if they go to the North Pole. Don't ask me why he wants to go to the North Pole.

'What a day,' Mum said, flopping on the settee. 'I can hardly move a muscle. Make me a cuppa, honey, and set the table. I've got a Parish Council meeting at 8.00 and the baby-sitter will be here before then so I've got to get organised.'

'It's all meetings for you, Mum, don't you do anything socially?' I enquired, picking the remainder of the chips off the floor.

'That's social.'

'But you don't meet any men.'

'I've seen enough of men during the day at work and then when I come home there's you two men.' Hell, Karen, she made us sound like dragons.

'You're not involved . . .'

'I'm not eighteen, you know,' she snapped. 'I'd like to see you at age forty getting involved. We old people can't go to discotheques, you know.'

'Life begins at forty.'

'Well, it would seem it does for your father.'

This was said with all the fire and passion she had left inside her.

'And so it should for you . . .'

'Jason, will you leave my sex life alone? I don't want to talk.'

She never talked with me. Kept it all inside; hell, it wasn't often I tried to prise it out. But I wanted her to stay alive, not rot away in her rocking chair. She's still so pretty, Karen, but she doesn't care.

I set out the table for three and then on seeing the chips I took my place away. I didn't feel hungry and I was too nervous to eat anyway.

'Meal's up,' I called and I started serving Ed, who could eat fish and chips until they came out of his ears. Mum slouched off the settee, hung her coat up and sat down at the table. On seeing I wasn't eating she looked up at me, displaying her nasty look.

'Why aren't you eating?'

I could tell she was mad because of the way she sucked her lips in.

'I'm not hungry,' I said firmly.

'You've been eating crisps and chocolate again ... I've told you not to ...'

'I haven't eaten nothing.'

'You mean "I haven't eaten anything". Well, you must be ill, a grown boy not eating his tea. Let me feel your head.'

How fussy she was, Karen. If you didn't eat a ton of food, she'd think you'd got some killer disease, and it's out with a thermometer and into bed with a glass of hot milk.

'Leave me alone, Mum.'

'I'll have yours,' said Ed, whose face had lit up at the prospect of more grub.

'I expect it's out to the pub tonight, out boozing with your mates.'

'No, I'm going to a disco with a girl.'

She was taken aback.

'A discotheque?' (She sounded like a real snob, when she said it that way). 'Aren't they a bit quiet for you? I thought they were Karen's haunts, not yours. Well at least they won't have any of your rock music there.'

'They won't have too much Manto-bloody-vani either,' I replied. Oh no, I thought, we've got another argument coming up.

'Manto-bloody-vani, as you so nicely put it, does come up with melodies and something resembling a tune, he also doesn't produce obscene and filthy lyrics.'

She stood up in anger, putting her hands on her hips. She was formidable like this. I wasn't in the mood to be put down all the same and I too stood up, leaving only Ed sitting down.

'You're a ..., a ...'

'Go on, say what you want. Call me anything you like.' She was shrieking it in a high voice and I could see tears in her eyes, but she'd never have admitted it.

I said nothing. It was at moments like that that I wanted

to get away from Mum. That was when I envied your cosy position, away from it all.

I left the room.

'I'm getting changed.'

I didn't need this, Karen. Nothing was going to spoil my evening, not that night of all nights. This was to be the one night where not one thing went wrong. It took me ages to prepare, I didn't know what to wear, a red shirt and white pullover or a stripey sweatshirt. The sweatshirt won on the toss of the coin. I cleaned my teeth so hard that my gums bled leaving a sour taste in my mouth. Then it was on with the body deodorant and aftershave. I even, wait for it, polished my shoes, an amazing feat as I hadn't worn the things for a year let alone polished them. I always wore trainers for school, but I sussed out that shoes would give me much needed class, as well as an inch or two. Having done everything, I looked at myself in the bathroom mirror and wondered why I'd been unfortunate enough to have the face that I did. It was an unusual face, the sort that some girls would like and some wouldn't. 'A face that was bound to turn some girl on,' you said in one of your amiable moods. That was nice, Karen, not that I really go for it. I'd have settled for a boring, handsome face like Lenny's that night.

I remember dreading going downstairs because I knew I'd have to tell Mum what time I'd be in. So I listened to records until 7.15 and then I had to go because I was meeting Hannah any time after 8.00. I saw Mum watching TV.

'I'll be back by 11.30,' I said sternly, not looking at her face. I tried to walk out without having to listen to her answer but she called quite loud, so I couldn't ignore her.

'Jason!'

'Yeah,' I blew out, expecting her to hammer me.

'Nice aftershave you've got on.'

'How can you tell from there?'

'Honey, they can probably smell you coming at the discotheque.'

'That strong, huh?'

'But very sexy!'

Ah Karen, was that her way of saying sorry? I was glad, because we were at least 'friends' again.

I got to Al's early, too early. I considered going to a pub to have a drink in order to ease my nerves. I didn't go, though, because I thought Hannah might smell the beer on my breath and be put off. That's how careful I was, Karen.

So I went in, passing the not so pleasant bouncer with a permanent sneer on his face. It was real trendy, Karen, I expect you'd have liked it. The place was almost full of couples, very debonaire guys with flashy girls in tight fitting trousers and glittery outfits. I felt like an odd one out, as if I was still wearing my brushed denim and my trainers. I had an uneasy feeling that I didn't fit in.

I'd never been to Al's before; you know I have been to a few discos in my time but not that one. I saw it as the type of place you went to with your friends. And Mum and Dad encouraged you to go because they had aspirations for you as a professional dancer. My guess is that you went as much to get picked up by some sweet-talking boy as to improve your dancing. Cast your mind back to your pre-Simon days when success was counted by the number of boys who'd ask you to dance. Don't forget those times, Karen.

It was real sweaty in there. Dark as well, the only lights in the place were the flashing ones for the disco and the elegantly decorated lamps that lit up the bar and the sides. In a way I was pleased it was so dark because no one would spot my dancing.

I decided to sit down at one of the tables by the bar and wait for Hannah. It was still only 8.00 and I was pleased to have the time on my own, in order to pull myself together. All I did was twiddle my thumbs and listen to the jerk DJ, he was a carbon copy of Colin (whoops sorry, Zeb).

'All right all you disco freakeroos, let's see you all boogying and getting on down to this disc . . . The Jacksons. And this is for Sally West, aged twenty, whose birthday it is tomorrow. Congratulations there, Sally baby, and maybe I can buy you a drink later.'

How could you stick those guys, Karen?

By the time 8.30 arrived, Hannah still hadn't come. I kept looking at the entrance, thinking every girl that walked in would be Hannah. Lucy arrived with a group of her girly friends. She saw me sitting at the table and came over to see me. She was in one of her bouncy, excitable moods.

'Jay,' she said, as if she was excited to see me, 'glad you came.'

'Oh, hullo Lucy.'

She was all glittery and silky, with beads and things round her hair. Looked like you, in all her trendy clothes.

'Isn't Hannah here yet?'

'No, I haven't seen her.'

'Oh don't panic. Hannah's always late, without fail. In fact most girls are, you should know that. She's looking forward to seeing you, I was talking to her on Wednesday and she's wild about you. Strange taste she's got.'

'You've said that before.'

'Only kidding, Jay. Well, I hope she arrives soon and puts a smile on your face.'

'Yeah.'

'Cheer up, you'll have a fun time,' she cheered and then one of her trendy friends pulled her by the arm. 'I'll catch you later, we're going to dance.' She started boogying towards the dance floor, simultaneously chattering as she went.

After that little interlude, I had nothing to do. I bought a drink to keep me occupied. You'll crack up when I tell you what I got. A tomato juice! All right, I only did it because I wasn't boozing.

Soon I was ordering a second and then a third and a fourth. I waited and waited, I had to keep asking people the time. And still she didn't come. In all my worst fears I'd never considered her not turning up. Sure, in my uneasy moments I'd feared her walking out on me because I was a bad dancer or she didn't like me. But I couldn't believe her not coming in the first place. Surely she couldn't do that to me; you'd never have done it, Karen. All I could do was sit on and on at the same table, watching people have a wild time, while I despairingly hoped.

Ah, hope! It was stupid and naive of me to wait as long as I did. I left Al's at 10.00; on my own outside a disco at 10.00 in the centre of town. It was very quiet outside, the silence only broken by the passing of the occasional bus or car. I walked around in circles, which I tend to do when I'm all confused. I genuinely do walk in circles, Karen, it's no joke. Eventually I went to the chippie at the bottom of the road, at least it was warm in there. I ordered a load of chips which I didn't really want off an old lady who obviously found it difficult to move. There was one other person in the chippie, a coloured guy who reminded me of those kids who'd duffed me up at the arcade. He was leaning against the wall saying nothing and looking pretty stoned. It was depressing, Karen, everything was depressing. I wished I'd drunk something now, like a bottle of whisky.

Those chips were horrible, the greasiest, squashiest chips you could imagine. I wasn't hungry anyway. I chucked the whole bag in the bin in disgust and started thinking about getting home. Then I heard these drunken voices behind me, singing some sort of song which I couldn't suss out.

'Jason,' called out the girl. I hardly recognised her until she got closer by the street lights and then I saw the beads in her hair. I'd never seen Lucy Norton, respectable Lucy Norton, pissed before. Normally I would have thought it funny but not then. She was with this hunk that went to Cartland, I knew him from the football team but I could never remember his name.

'Oh, hi ...' I said, trying like hell to be sociable.

'You're not in the disco, Jason,' slurred Lucy, her words all mumbled up.

'No Lucy, very observant. I'm eating chips or I was until I threw them away.'

'Oh dear,' she said, and she pulled my cheeks vigorously. 'And Hannah's let you down, what a silly girl. How could anyone do that to you? Never mind, Jason. That's Hannah for you. Hey Jay, you've met Peter.'

'Hi.'

'Lucy,' I said, 'what do you mean, Hannah's like that? Like what?'

She belched and then giggled.

'Oh, I don't know, she's unpre . . . dicable.'

'She means UNPREDICTABLE,' said Peter helpfully. That didn't help me at all. Unpredictable could mean anything. You and I are unpredictable, but we still turn up to discos when we've arranged to. All she managed to do by saying that was get me even more confused. I didn't know what to think, Karen. I felt kind of desperate, like I didn't quite know what to do.

'Peter . . . the world's going round . . . look, you're going round.' This Peter kid put his arm round her waist and practically held her up. She was tanked up to the brim. Peter had achieved part of his aim. Another stud, I couldn't get away from them. Next, he was going to take her down some dark alley and unceremoniously screw her. Oh dear, Karen, am I being cynical again? Sorry, I expect he took her home that night, gave her a goodnight kiss and went away. Yeah, that's what he did. Right? I shook my head and went home.

TWELVE

I stewed during the weekend. I kept wondering about Hannah. I considered giving her a phone call. I nearly even gave you a call to ask for your advice (well, I didn't have the Samaritans' phone number). But in the end, I decided to go and see her on Monday. Oh, that Monday was something else, Karen.

It was early Monday morning that I got startling news. Me and the lads were talking, as we did. Justin was probing me about what happened at the disco.

'It was fine,' I said.

'We were all saying how funny it would be if you went to the crap disco and the bird didn't turn up.'

'Oh.'

'How much did she let you have, Jay?' Bones asked eagerly.

'Not a lot.' Jay Border wins first prize for understatement of the year.

'Ah birds, they're like that on the first date.'

I wouldn't know, Karen. I hadn't got as far as the first date. As we talked, Carl came up from the other side of the main hall. I could tell something was wrong. He was jolly on principle, even in the mornings.

'Cookie's been in an accident. He's seriously ill.'

We looked at each other, this was the kind of thing that never happened to me. I mean, people I knew never got seriously hurt. I didn't know what death meant, I read about it in the papers or saw it on the TV, but that was it.

'Bloody hell.'

'I don't believe it,' said Bones.

'He got knocked over by a bus, would you credit it? Helena told me about it, she said she saw it happen, he walked straight in front without looking. Crazy.'

'Maybe he did see it coming.'

'Come again?'

'Well, I'm saying that perhaps he did look, and that's why he walked out.'

Should I have said that, Karen? I figured that I was right about it, but it was less than tactful. Carl reacted.

'Rembrandt, you amaze me. A kid has an accident and you want to dramatise it by building it into an attempted suicide. We're not playing cowboys and Indians here, it's real life.'

'Don't patronise me, Carl.'

'All right, we won't talk about it then.'

'OK.'

And we went all silent. Then Marshall appeared, thinking he was the first to tell everyone the news.

'Cookie's been in a bus accident. What a twat. He got knocked over in the middle of town. Trust Cookie.'

'We know,' said Justin.

'And we're not talking about it,' Carl added.

'Oh,' Marshall sounded disappointed.

'Hadn't we better sent him a card or something?' Justin said. 'It would be nice.'

'Don't bother. My guess is he'll be out in a couple of days,' Marshall remarked. A compassionate lad he was. 'He's got a maths test on Thursday and his Dad won't want him to miss it ...' It was supposed to be a joke, but for once no one laughed, not Justin, or Bones or Carl. It was very quiet, everyone looked down at the floor. Can you picture it, Karen? In the end, Carl broke the tension.

'You should've been at the pub on Friday night.'

'Yeah, Jay, it was really ace. Tom Barron came down and he got really pissed. And then he starts flirting with these girls and he got chucked out. Everyone was laughing at him.'

'He'll be walking in front of a bus next,' I said spitefully.

No one caught on except Carl but he said nothing. Justin and Marshall carried on telling me this terrific story. I listened but that was all, I kept thinking about Cookie.

It was the guilt I felt more than anything. I blamed myself for what had happened to him. Those things he told me about people laughing at each other. We were all to blame, Karen, the whole bunch of us.

This won't surprise you. The lads didn't send a card. 'Too much hassle,' as Marshall might have put it. Might ruin that famous image. Of all his friends, I was the only one to visit him. That says it all.

And I committed the crime of all crimes, Karen, according to the hospital staff. I went to see him after school not in 'official' visiting hours. Like I told the receptionist, I didn't know it all had to be so official. I got to see him, though. 'Two minutes only please, sir.'

Well, how nice of them. I bought him some chocolates because when people go to see people in hospital they bring stuff, don't they? Most people bring grapes, Mum made me bring you grapes when you had appendicitis. 'Jay Border,' I thought, 'would you want a bunch of grapes or a box of chocolates if you were stuck in a hospital bed?' Mind you, when I saw the kid I realised he wouldn't want chocolate or grapes.

'Here he is,' said the nurse who took me to him. He was in the seventh or eighth bed along in his ward. I didn't recognise him, partly because he didn't have his glasses on. He was so messed up that I wouldn't have recognised him anyway. He was covered in bandages, it was incredible. And his head, Karen, it was terrible. He had this enormous bruise just below his right eye which had swelled so that he could hardly open it. He had cuts and nicks all over him, Karen, and he was under sedation. I couldn't believe that anyone with that number of injuries could still be alive. It made me ill to look at him; he was horribly mutilated.

'Cooks,' I said quietly, moving slowly closer to him.

'Jay?' he questioned. His voice was almost too low to hear, the words were strained.

'Yeah, I thought I'd pop in to see you. I've brought you some chocs, for later on. I don't suppose you've got too much of an appetite.'

He tried to shake his head. Every movement was hard. I was shocked.

'Uh . . . the lads send you their best.' I didn't know what to say next. 'They all said they'd have come but they've got football practice and things on. I see you've got lots of cards from family and stuff.'

'Yes.'

'So what a daft thing to do, huh, Cookie?' I said, trying to instil some humour into the conversation. The lad's practically a vegetable, yet Jay still cracks the jokes.

He answered me, in short breaths.

'I had . . . too much drink.'

'I didn't know you were drinking on Friday night. You weren't with the lads that night, I know. Who were you with?'

'No one.'

'Drinking alone, Cookie!' I said, all surprised. It may not seem that odd to you, Karen, but Cookie never drank alone and on top of that he didn't usually drink too much. It was one of the 'in' jokes that Cookie never drank more than two pints, though he had gone over that a bit recently. 'Cookie, you shouldn't drink alone, I asked you to come to the disco.'

'I know,' he murmured.

OK, Karen. I said another dumb thing. You're right, I shouldn't have mentioned it, but I had to share the guilt.

'Cookie, I think you deliberately walked in front of the bus.'

He smiled.

'Now would I do that?'

'Yes.'

'Well, let's say that if I did . . . it would have been partly due to drink.'

I'd known it all along.

'Hey man, don't you do that again.'

'Course not . . . don't worry, Jay.'

The nurse came and told me it was time to leave and that Cookie needed some sleep.

'You hang in there,' I said.

He smiled again. I felt terrible and more guilty than when I went in. I had all these doubts about him making it, even though the nurse had told me he was well on his way to recovery. I thought of his Dad putting pressure on him and the lads teasing him. And if he did make it, would he do the same thing over again? Perhaps he'd succeed next time. I really wanted him to make it, I'd never had close friends and Cookie wasn't especially close, but if people like him didn't make it we'd be left with self-proclaimed survivors like Marshall and Bones and everyone else. But what about me, was I like them or Cookie? I used to be like the lads, but now I detest them. You tell me where I belong, Karen, because I'll be damned if I know.

THIRTEEN

It was a visit that shook me, Karen, a visit that helped to shake me out of my self-contented, relatively happy-go-lucky shoes. All those things you'd hammered me for. My insensitivity, selfishness, lack of compassion; every one of those descriptions fitted me. And I thought it was only 'big sister' getting heated for the sake of it. Sixteen years old and the penny's finally dropped.

It all happened in that one week; Cookie and Hannah. For five minutes while I was in that hospital, I miraculously stopped thinking about the girl. But the moment I came out I switched back to her as if I was switching channels on television.

On Tuesday I did eventually see her. I had to wait until lunchtime before I got the chance, but I found out what I needed to know before then. It was at that place beside the coats and by the window overlooking the fields. I was talking to the lads as usual. Always talking to the lads, what a bore, huh? This time they wanted to know about Cookie, more out of morbid excitement than sympathy. I thought they were like a bunch of news reporters searching for a good story.

'He's badly knocked, but he'll be OK.'

'It's bad. You can't believe it when it happens to someone you know,' said Carl. He was the one kid who did seem genuinely knocked back by it. I couldn't see why, Karen. He never seemed to understand Cookie. Hey, maybe he was on a guilt trip like me.

'Ah well, that's life,' Justin added, needless to say not

exactly knocked back by the accident. 'Hey, Jay, have you done that homework?'

'What homework?'

'History,' he sighed.

I looked frantically in my bag and pulled out my battered looking history folder. I hadn't done it.

'Shit!'

'Your work-rate's about nil,' sneered Justin.

'Oh I'm very sorry, teacher. I'm glad to see you're so concerned about my work-rate, I'll try to improve.'

'If you fail your exams don't run to me,' he laughed. That sounded like you, Karen (horror of horrors). The reminder of what a layabout I was. It was true that I'd hardly worked those weeks, with Hannah on my mind.

'Hey, Rembrandt, here comes Lucy.'

'Oh yes, you should've seen her Friday night ...' I whispered. 'She was ...'

Before I could finish she was right beside me so I shut up. She was with her usual posse of friends.

'Jay, can I have a moment?'

'Sure.'

'Alone!' she emphasised.

I knew what she was going to say, Karen. I can't usually read you birds like you apparently can read me, but I had an idea of what was coming up.

'Hannah doesn't want to go out with you.'

She said it straight, no pulled punches. I really couldn't believe it. I didn't feel anything except total numbness, it was a strange, empty sort of thing. In all honesty, Karen, the significance of her words hadn't sunk in. Was it the same when Simon first told you? I bet you were speechless, Karen. I can see it now.

'That's OK, is it?' she said.

'Yes ... no. Of course it isn't. She hasn't even explained why.'

'You're not going to like this.'

'Tell me.'

'Her old boyfriend asked her out on Friday evening, so she

94

went with him. I'm sorry, I would've told you yesterday but I didn't want to have to be the one to have to break it.'

'Yeah.'

'That's what she's like, Jay. I'm sorry.'

'It's OK.'

It wasn't. She left me in a state of utter disbelief. I thought it was the guy that was meant to do this thing to girls, not the other way round. Hell, Karen, when he chucked you, he had the nerve to tell you himself. I had it by message. You girls are the same as us. We're all as bad as each other. That crap about girls being more gentle and caring than boys is a myth. Don't forget that, ever, Karen.

'What's up, Rembrandt?'

I hadn't realised Carl and Marshall had joined me.

'Your bird chucked you?' Carl said.

'Yeah.'

'Wow, I was only kidding.'

'Ah, never mind,' I said, probably unconvincingly. 'There's more where she came from.' I didn't mean it.

'That's right. They're practically everywhere. You can't keep away from them,' said Marshall in his assured voice again.

'That's the way it goes,' said Carl, all philosophical. I didn't feel very philosophical, shattered I felt. Shattered and numbed.

So, one teenage love affair bites the dust. Love affair, that's funny. I felt like I'd been through it all, yet we'd not even got off the ground. I figured there wasn't quite enough material for a Mills and Boon romance. You know, Karen, you should savour those three weeks, four days, eleven hours and thirty three minutes that you shared with good old Simon. So it ended, but if you loved him as much as I know you did, it must have been so special.

Stupidly, I couldn't accept it was over. Sane, normal people would have left things as they were, but not me. I went to see her that lunchtime.

I decided to go to the park, remembering the time I'd seen her there. Sure enough she was there, on the exact same bench with the same beige coat. She wasn't alone this time, her boyfriend was there. She looked so different with another boy, I'd always thought of her with me. He was better looking than me, but I guessed that he was probably the type that wore through birds like they were clothes. When he got bored with them he'd throw them away and get a new one. Oh I expect he was all right, Karen, I was jealous, that's all. You know what he was doing? Eating her sandwiches. Hey, do you think if I'd have eaten her mum's sarnies she'd have liked me more? Well, it was an idea.

I spied at them from the edge of the park, by the road, watching their every move. And then I heard this voice beside me.

'Bird-watching are we, Jay? The feathered variety, of course.' It was the unmistakable gruff voice of a lad I knew at Jenny High called Geoff.

'Oh, hi Geoff,' I said, pretending to be pleased to see him. 'I haven't seen you in yonks.'

'I've been busy at work, mate. Beaut laugh, working at the garage.'

'Good.'

'I've got a new bike and all. Second-hand you know, I bought it off my brother's mate a week ago last Monday. Only £40, mind you I've had to do it up a bit.'

'That's really terrific.' More bike talk, I really didn't want to talk bikes at a time like this, Karen.

'See this paintwork here.' He pointed to his engine. 'It was a mess before; I did it up in purple. It's fixed and looking great now.'

'Terrific.'

'How much do you think I can get out of it?'

'I haven't a clue. Fifty?'

'No.'

'Sixty?'

'No chance.'

96

We could have been there all day, Karen. I hadn't got all day.

'You tell me.'

'Sixty-seven, outdoes my mate's.'

'Hey look, Geoff. I've got to get back to school soon, so I'd better rush,' I said, trying to break the conversation. I was terrified I'd miss my chance of seeing Hannah. In the corner of my eye, I saw her stud boyfriend kiss her goodbye and go off. She was alone now.

'Maybe we could get together for a drink sometime,' I said all friendly as I walked away from him.

'Yeah, that'd be great. I'll look forward to it.'

'See you,' I said and breathed a sigh of relief. I was now travelling on the path that would take me to where she was sitting. I was totally psyched up for this, my mind was only on her and what I'd say. As I came close she became clearer, she looked the same as she'd always been, her soft hair, her dazzling eyes, the relaxed look. But somehow it was all different.

She saw me when I was about twenty yards away. She was surprised, I could tell.

'Can we talk?'

'I suppose.'

I ushered her towards the football fields indicating I wanted a walk. I pointed where I wanted to go, but was careful not to touch her in any way. I saw my hand shaking. I wasn't used to this type of thing. Making sentimental pleas wasn't the way I spent my spare time. I'm sure I approached the whole thing wrong, Karen. Tell me, what does the guy do when he's trying to tell a girl a hundred things which really mean he needs her? For once in my life, I spoke from the heart. Tell me if that was a mistake, Karen.

'Well, you wanted to talk,' she said almost sharply. It was as if she didn't know what I was going to say. 'Go ahead.'

'OK ... I want an explanation.'

'What for?' she said naively. Her large eyes looked questioningly.

'Well, for starters there's the disco. You didn't even tell me you weren't coming. And then I hear about this boyfriend. How could you let me down, Hannah?'

'Who do you think I am?' she stormed. 'I've got the right to do what I want, or I should have. I don't want to be used.'

She sounded like you, Karen. I'd never seen her annoyed. It disturbed me.

'Lucy said you liked me; I thought you liked me, that's all.'

'I did like you, Jason ... quite a lot. But you're not the only person I've fancied, or ever will. If you'd have asked me out earlier it might have been another thing. But Steven and I know each other well and we're together now. I'm sorry.'

She was more sympathetic.

'I care for you,' I said.

'I know,' she smiled. 'Don't work yourself up over it, Jason, it's silly. In no time you'll meet another girl, someone nicer than a supermarket assistant who doesn't turn up for dates.'

Oh Karen, as if I cared who she was, or what she was, or where she came from.

'I want you.'

'Sorry Jason,' her voice was soft and touching. 'I am sorry.'

And then she placed her hand gently at the side of my face and kissed me delicately on the cheek. It meant everything to me, Karen, I felt cold and passionate, I shivered at the beauty of it. I'll never forget it.

'It was nice knowing you, Jason.'

'Yes,' I swallowed. I watched her walk away from me for the last time. I felt the moistness of tears in my eyes. I held them back.

'I love you, Hannah, I love you,' I said time after time under my breath. I felt desperate then, nothing was worth it any more. I wanted to die, let me die, Karen.

FOURTEEN

Ah, suicide, Karen. It's a fantasy, a way out. That's all, though. Hell, you said you wanted to do it; but it never happened. Cookie did try, I'll give him that. But what happens to him? He pisses it up and ends up in hospital with a battered face.

Oh I know, Karen, for the classic ending to this story it would have been more fitting if I'd got myself run over by a lorry or something. But hard luck, it didn't happen like that for me. Instead I went back to school and sat through the lessons and talked to the lads and went home to Mum and Ed. And all that routine was worse and more unbearable than it had ever been. And there was no one to talk to, to cry to. I kept it all inside.

That following week was the one where we had the students. Those poor bloody students. Only your age, yet they put up with self-satisfied saps who think they know it all, knocking lumps out of them. We had two that term, Karen, Mr Smith and Mr Lynam. Mr Smith was lucky, full of confidence, very handsome. You birds swoon at people with his looks, 'Oh he's so gorgeous, I could scream'. Mr Lynham wasn't so fortunate as Smithy. He was visibly scared out of his wits at seeing us, incredibly nervous he was. I felt sorry for him. You know on the first day he taught us he introduced himself and started teaching the lesson, and all the time he had his flies down. He thought everyone was laughing at him, which they were in the end. He'll never teach sixth form again after his experience here, I'm sure of that.

'I can't believe how bad he is. It's an embarrassment,'

Carl noted as we came out of the lesson. 'His hand shook as he wrote on the blackboard.'

'Yeah, and when he told that joke and no one laughed, he went all red,' Bones added.

I did try to defend him, Karen, in a weak sort of way.

'He's scared out of his wits.'

'Yeah, I know, Rembrandt. The guy's a wreck, he shouldn't be here.'

'Makes for entertaining lessons,' sneered Bones. 'Hey and you know Sandy's invited him to the party on Saturday night. For a joke, I reckon.'

I hadn't heard about this party, although I knew Sandy Maple had one about this time of year. We got invited as well, she must have been mad. Well, would you have invited us to a party? No, I thought not.

'Are you going, lads?' I asked.

'Of course we are, Rembrandt, Sandy's parties bring back sweet memories. Me and Stella in the back bedroom.'

Carl didn't keep his conquests secret, in fact I heard from somewhere that he was about to get them published in paperback. Not that it would be a super-enormous book.

'Shut up, Carl.'

'Ah, memories,' he continued.

'You are coming?' Bones said. 'It's tradition, and it'll help you forget about your old flame. There's always booze and birds at Sandy's. It's great fun.'

'Yeah ... I suppose I'll be there,' I sighed.

I supposed that a wild night might buck me up and I'd forget Hannah 'for evermore'. I thought, 'no way am I going to lock myself up like Karen did. I'm going to forget.' That somewhat naive thought came from another time, when I was depressed. I never told you about it, did I? It was a year ago and I'd argued with Mum about something trivial. That night I was feeling so down that I got totally pissed. And I felt so good, Karen, happy as you like. But it didn't happen this time round. I suppose you could have predicted it, huh?

Even before this party, we had to get all psyched up, so

that we were jolly and extrovert. The lads that night were all fun-loving and spruced up. I was pretending to be the same, but inside I was a wet rag. Hell, I didn't even bother to put my aftershave on.

So there we were walking to Sandy's, about six of us, looking a right bunch of jerks with crates of beer and bottles in our hands. Discussing the possibilities of the evening, that's what we were doing. 'I fancy my luck with such and such a girl.' 'Who do you fancy yours with?' 'Oh, I don't know, I'll suss the scene out.'

And then we got there, to be greeted cheerfully by Sandy in her cute red boiler suit and a glass of Martini in her hand.

'Oh, hullo boys, how nice of you to come.'

In we pile, crashing in and 'sussing the scene out', as we might say. Usually I'd be slightly nervous at the beginning of a party, what with all the people and the need to talk and chat up. This time, though, I wasn't nervous at all, I didn't care.

It was your average party. You've been to millions of them yourself. A record player on one side of the large living room with a bunch of kids trying to put their own records on it. A space to dance if you wished, which hardly anyone did. Chairs and sofas pushed to the side. Does this ring a bell, Karen? To get a drink you went into the kitchen which smelt of stale alcohol and was cramped with people pretending to be completely gone. A smoke-filled, darkened orgy, that's all it was.

At the early part of the 'orgy' it was very respectable. Guys trying to make intellectual conversation with girls, about their hobbies and how they were enjoying school. The girlies looking very cute and 'nice'; that would change by the end of the evening.

The moment I walked into the party I knew my heart wasn't into it, which is disastrous for this kind of thing. There was only one girl that meant anything to me, all the rest were secondary. Well, I thought. You came for one thing, drown your sorrows.

I went to get a drink in the kitchen. I smiled pleasantly at people that I knew not so well and they smiled back. Marshall was in there, smoking.

'Hey, Marshall,' I said. 'Give us a fag.'

I didn't smoke except at parties. That's no lie, Karen. It was a social thing, to ease nerves or whatever.

'Yeah, sure. Good party, huh?'

'It sure is.'

He bumped into some plump kid and spilt his beer all over the kitchen floor and me. Terrific, eh, Karen? The fool's got the whole house to spill his beer on, and he throws it over me.

'Soz, Jay.'

'Doesn't matter.'

'I'll see you later on. Don't do what I wouldn't do.'

I got my glass of wine and drank it straight. It was disgusting, I felt my throat burn. Real plonk it was. I still grabbed a second glass though and I took it back into the living room, careful not to spill it as I went.

There was a space on the sofa near the kitchen door, so I took it. On my right was Bones trying to chat up some girl he'd liked for ages. In front of me was a gathering of kids sitting in a circle, cross-legged. They had a bottle with them, and seemed to be having a fun time. I looked to my left, Jane Carter was alone. In fact, she looked sad. She had a purple V-necked jumper on with her jeans. She was pretty, Karen. Very tender and open. I hardly knew her. I think she did sciences. Now Karen, you've got to believe me when I tell you that I didn't want to chat her up. She was alone, though, so I figured that it wouldn't do any harm to talk to her.

'Nice party,' I said.

'Yes.'

'What are you drinking?'

'Some of Sandy's punch. I'm not sure what's in it.'

'Oh, I've taken some of the cheap wine she's got in here.'

'You got any fags?' she said to me.

'No,' I anwered, puffing mine away. 'I got this one from Marshall. You do sciences, don't you?'

'Yes, that's right, Chemistry, Physics and Maths.'

'Must be tough.'

'It's not too bad, a lot of work though.'

Have you noticed that we skipped through three or four major talking points in fifteen seconds? I often found that when you hardly knew the bird you were talking to the subject matter kept changing. Loads of little clichéd phrases like 'nice dress you're wearing,' or 'nice day today, isn't it?' I'm sure we guys are totally predictable.

'Here, get me another will you?' She thrust her glass at me. 'I can't be bothered to go myself. Ta.'

'Yeah, what'll you have?'

'Same again.'

'Uh-huh, that punch must be good.'

I don't usually think I'm well in with a girl but for some reason I thought I was with this one. It was one of my hunches, Karen. But the irony of the thing was that for once it didn't mean anything to me. I didn't want to be in with her, I wanted Hannah, is that so strange? I simply wasn't turned on or anything else by Jane, even if I'd have wanted to be. I decided to get drunk, maybe that would change my mood.

We talked and drank for ages. Too long really; I was talking because I didn't want to do anything else. It was a strain, Karen. We were talking about her horse riding whilst all around us were getting stuck in, for want of better words. I felt as if I had to do the same, despite not wanting to. Everyone else was doing it, I didn't want to be the one next morning to say I hadn't got off with a girl. Yeah, very immature of me, isn't it, Karen?

But this was a farce. I felt awkward. In the end I put my arm around her. It felt mechanical, but she still drew closer to me. She was eager to kiss and that, but I was sitting there, half drunk and not wanting to do it. I started to kiss her, slow and long. I might as well have been kissing the sofa. All of a sudden I felt totally impotent. So now I'm a freak, Karen.

'Excuse me,' I said breaking off, 'I've got to go to the toilet.'

I had to get away, Karen, I wanted to run as far away as possible. I ran through the kitchen grabbing a bottle as I went and was out of the back door before anyone could notice.

It was foggy outside, I ran by the road as if I was jogging in the evening. Every now and again I'd stop to swallow from the bottle, it must have been whisky or gin, I didn't know.

It wasn't like last time I'd got drunk, I felt desperate. It was supposed to have helped me, but the booze made me worse, it was driving me mad, I couldn't control the anger and bitterness inside me. Instead of jogging I broke into a run, my head shaking from side to side, I think I went past two skinheads. They were laughing at me, that's all I can remember. I was past them in a second, still running, towards the park.

City Park was a full two miles away from Sandy's but I got there in no time. I don't think I'd consciously gone there. It was lifeless and empty, totally quiet. I could hear the sound of my breath. As my eyes got accustomed to the dark I saw the bench where I'd last spoken to Hannah. I stumbled towards it, I was so mad and mixed up that I was half-expecting to see her there. I kept repeating her name.

At the bench I fell, the bottle smashed on the ground and I felt my body hit the moist surface. I tried to get up, but there wasn't the strength or will. It was the worst feeling I've ever had, I was uncontrollably depressed. Can you truly understand the depth of the anger and hopelessness of it, Karen?

I was crying in the middle of a deserted park with no one to help me. I half expected you to appear and place your hand on my shoulder, as I did to you after Simon. Do you remember that, Karen? Oh, I know I didn't understand why you felt so very, very bad; but I was there. No one was within miles of me. That loneliness still haunts me.

FIFTEEN

The ninth miracle of the world was that I somehow managed to get home. I don't know how, I never will. Maybe I walked, but it's all a void. I woke up on the floor at the bottom of our stairs. My clothes were wet and I felt uncomfortable. My head was aching and I was real thirsty. I felt weak and strained as a result of the previous night.

The smell of cooking bacon woke me. Yeah, Mum is cooking bacon and eggs to this very day. Ed, still in his Action Man pyjamas, crept up behind me and booted me, like the little charmer that he was. I groaned.

'Mummy says you've got to get up.'

I turned over.

'Why are you sleeping here?'

'Don't ask.'

I wasn't exactly going to tell a six-year-old kid why I got in late last night. So instead, I stumbled off the settee and creaked towards the kitchen. I was fully prepared for the hammering I expected Mum to give me. She was listening to some twat on the radio who sounded all jolly when I walked in. He was going on about what a lovely morning it was; it was a pain.

'Morning,' I muttered. Mum was poised over the cooker, turning the bacon over. She was in one of those elegant silk night gowns. But her hair was messy and her face more strained than usual.

She didn't reply to me, didn't even look at me.

'You cooking bacon?'

'For myself and Edward, you can make your own.'

Wow, was she annoyed, I can't remember the last time she hadn't cooked me breakfast. I don't blame her though.

'I don't want any, I feel too ill.'

'Surprise, surprise,' she whispered tautly under her breath.

'My head's killing me, Mum. Where's the aspirin?'

'Bathroom. You've already had one, when you came in at three o'clock.'

She really emphasised the three o'clock bit to make me feel extra guilty, which I did. I thought she was going to say 'Karen never came in as late as 3.00.' Luckily she didn't.

'It was that late, huh?' I said humbly.

'I rang Sandra's house at 1.00 when you hadn't arrived home. She had no idea where you were. So I rang up all your friends, waking up half the parents in the process. Then I went out looking for you in the car but I couldn't find you. I waited up until 3.00, I was scared stiff you'd been killed.'

Her face said it all.

'Ah, Mum, you shouldn't worry about me ...'

'Three o'clock, and you woke Edward with your drunken singing and your shouting. Smelling of sewage water.'

'It wasn't sewage water.'

She shouted painfully, 'Whatever it is, the stuff's all over the living room.'

I didn't know what to say, Karen. I guess I could have apologised.

'I'll get an aspirin.'

'Oh ... I nearly forgot, a letter arrived for you and Edward. You weren't here, so I let Edward open it. It was an invitation to a wedding ...'

'Dad and Jill?'

She nodded and turned the bacon over again. She must have turned the bacon over at least fifty times in our conversation.

'24th of November.'

'Very fitting that it's twenty one years, almost to the day, since we got engaged.'

I looked at her sympathetically. Her face was without emotion.

'I'd . . . I'd have stayed at home if I'd known the letter was going to arrive last night.'

'I talked to Karen on the phone, a five minute call; she was on the way to a party so she couldn't talk for long.'

That pretty well summed up our connections with you. Five minutes on a crackly telephone line. I'm sure she felt much better after her super-long conversation with you. Hell, Karen, five lousy minutes! Well, I hope you had a rotten party.

I shrugged my shoulders and left her in the kitchen. Mum handled things better without me, it was you she could have done with.

Let's say I wasn't wildly energetic about going to school. Facing the 'morons' didn't appeal to me, I felt like I couldn't stick them any more. I wanted out from the group; all that attention-seeking and competing for popularity was unimportant now.

The question was, would I last the day without blowing up? The answer arrived early that day. Lenny was talking (well, Karen, what else did he do?) about a kid he'd got into a scrap with.

'My friends,' he said, 'this wog came up to me after geography class and told me that I got on his nerves. I couldn't believe it.'

'How could you possibly get on anyone's nerves?' I said dryly. Nobody listened to what I said.

'He walked up to me,' continued Lenny, 'and said I had too much to say. And I told him that it's better than staying quiet all lesson like he does. He never says anything, the wog. He sits for an hour like a stuffed dummy.'

'Probably a shy bastard,' said Justin as the bell went for the first lesson of the day. We all started moving out of the room, but Lenny hadn't finished yet so naturally we had to hear it out.

'So that's his hang-up. I thought wogs were meant to be all lively.'

'That's West Indians. Pakis are all quiet and nice,' said Justin, chewing his gum. Boy, did it annoy me, the way he chewed his gum.

'They're all trouble,' said Lenny dominantly. I looked around to see who might disagree with them. Almost everyone listening was laughing. 'More trouble than they're worth, Pakis. They come over here smelling of garlic, and then they nick our jobs.'

'If I was in charge,' said Justin, 'they'd all be out. Wogs, Pakis, all the Irish, the lot.'

This was getting to be a two-way convo between two pseudo-Nazis. Now don't tell me, Karen, that sixteen and seventeen-year-old kids in a sixth form, multi-racial college couldn't possibly be ignorant or insensitive enough to talk like this. They do, believe me.

In my normal, impassive mood I would have done what all the others did, laugh and agree. After all, I'd tell myself, talking about it wouldn't harm anyone. But I reacted that day; went crazy mad, as Carl put it.

'Sounds like you two are fascists.' I pointed accusingly at Lenny and Justin. They were taken aback and all the lads were surprised. For starters, no one challenged Lenny and also I never got into arguments. I could feel people around me laughing at the tension between me and Lenny.

'Jay, don't get narked, man. There's nothing wrong with being right-wing. There are a lot of people in the British Movement who are damned likeable people. I know loads of them myself.'

'Like who?'

'My brother's got a mate, Jazz Stone. Works down the factory. Great lad, I know him.'

Jazz Stone was a nut, Karen.

'He got done for kicking a Paki's head in.'

My voice was raised and I felt myself heating up.

'Oh Rembrandt, cool it,' said Carl.

'I don't want no political argument, Jay, all I'm saying is that the N.F. have a lot of fair ideas. So they hate wogs, seems fair enough.'

'I expect you're a subscribed member.'

'No space.'

'Too right, you're not. All you are is a phoney who likes watching the N.F. in the scraps on television. You make me sick.'

I was so strong, Karen. I laid it on him. I hardly knew I had it in me. I must have picked it up from you somewhere along the line. Lenny wasn't taken aback, though. He was totally calm which somehow made me look the fool in front of everyone.

'Well, would you credit it, Jay the nigger lover, the trendy left-winger. What a marvellous guy.'

I heard the teasing and the mocking from the lads, Carl and Justin and Lenny, all the people who'd been my friends for the past two or three years or more. Friends, that was a laughable term, it meant nothing to me. I walked away from them all.

Outside the school it was very quiet. Everyone was inside and going to lessons. On getting out there I hit the hell out of this metal post propped up by the science labs. My fists were whacking it, tearing and bruising the roots of my clenched knuckles. And when I finished, the pain ran through my hands. I expect I looked silly, but only Carl who was coming out of the main doors of the school saw me.

'I wondered where you were,' he said. 'We've got a lesson.'

'You go on.'

'I'll wait for you, come on.'

He stood there waiting for me, so I had to go towards him.

'Oh man, Rembrandt, did you go crazy mad. You were all steaming up, man.'

'I thought he was wrong.' Hell, Karen, I know he was wrong.

'It doesn't matter.'

'Of course it does. He'll go around for the rest of his life saying stuff like that. He's a pratt.'

'Rembrandt, listen to your Uncle Carl,' he sighed. 'There were people in there laughing at you.'

'Carl, they'll laugh at anything, it's not the point.'

'But it is.' Carl was too easy-going, he didn't mind what I thought. He was naive, Karen. 'Take it easy, Jay. Look around you ... laugh at things, you're too serious.'

I said nothing.

'Come on,' he added, 'let's go to the lesson and take the piss out of the students ...'

That was it, Karen. I'd had enough.

'No more,' I said, real serious. 'I've finished, I'm not coming back here again.'

And with that, I dropped my bag with all those precious books and notes that didn't mean a thing. I walked slowly out of that school, but I never once looked back. Behind me Carl was shouting to me.

'You're crazy, Jay, you're crazy.'

Crazy! I figured I was doing the only sane thing left open to me. I was sure I'd never go back to Cartland. You understand, don't you, Karen? No one else could see. Mum thought I was being 'impetuous' and the lads thought it was a stunt. But you'd have backed me up. I was truly right this time.

SIXTEEN

So here I was on a cold October morning, roughly 9.30. It was very strange, Karen. There were all these people in the city doing the things they had to do; business appointments, the morning shopping, catching the next bus. And there was good old me totally free to do what I wanted, and when. It was a vaguely happy sensation, but tinged with confusion.

'Hell,' I thought, 'now I've got my freedom what am I going to do with it?' There was always a job to consider, but what kind of job could I do in this type of mood? It turned out to be a day of loose ends, of walking round shops and parks searching for a way to kill time, of looking at clothes which were too expensive for me anyway, of sitting on park benches and watching nothing.

It took me twenty-five minutes to walk into the centre of town. No jogging this day, I took as long as possible. At about 10.15 I decided (now promise me you won't get over-excited about this) to go for a drink. What a thrill for me. I went into this cafe, a really spruced up one where the coffee was meant to be some special kind and where your sugar came in those little bags.

It was very empty and quiet in there. A dead atmosphere. I supposed that it was a bit early for morning coffee. This young woman served me, a right casual dame. She was leaning against the food display, half asleep.

'Hot chocolate, please.'

'30p, love,' she replied, pouring the drink practically everywhere except the cup.

'You can't charge 30p for that.'

'We can and will, it's inflation.'

'It's a rip-off.'

It was an extremely memorable conversation, probably because it was the only one I had with anyone for about five hours. Oh and after that, your 'immature' brother lived up to his name. To get my revenge for being ripped off 30p for a cup of chocolate I nicked fifteen bags of sugar and half a dozen metal spoons. So now I'm a criminal as well as a drop-out. It took me ages to finish off my drink. I made it last, because it was nice and warm inside. I found this newspaper on the seat where I was sat but I couldn't concentrate on it.

The highlight of this historic day was meeting my two mates Leonard and Winston in town. Yes, that's right; the 'awfully nice chaps' from the arcade. I bumped into them whilst in Woolworth's; they were dossing about like me.

'Hey, Leonard, it's the schoolboy.'

I was tempted to run away, but I didn't bother, so I faced up to them. Too much had happened, Karen; what did I care what they did now?

'Schoolboy, watcha doing here?'

'Looking at records,' I mentioned casually, pretending not to notice them.

'Why aren't you at school, boy?'

'I quit.'

They looked at each other, bemused.

'Why?'

'Who knows?'

These two jerks thought it was hysterically funny and started hitting each other's hands and shaking me by the hand.

'Hey man, join the club,' said one of them. 'The schoolboy is one of us.' And they laughed again. I was standing there wondering why all of a sudden I was a folk hero. It was amazing, Karen.

'You know what I'm going to do for you, *ex*-schoolboy? I is gonna buy you a hamburger.'

'Cheers.'

112

And he did too. It was funny in a crazy way. I expect they thought I was one of them now, the three million unemployed. But I wasn't, I knew that. They were OK, though, at least I didn't have to put on a false image for them. They knew what I was like.

What a weird day it was, Karen; I burnt my school jumper to make them happy and we went round the shops. And by the end of the afternoon they went home and I was alone again. Then came my hitch, I hadn't the nerve to get the bus home. Nothing to do with Hannah, I didn't take the 59 any more. The fact of it was I couldn't face Mum. How could I tell her I'd finished with school? It would be unthinkable for her, especially after how you'd progressed.

I got all these stupid ideas into my head that afternoon. I thought how great it might be if I was to leave the whole city and set up digs somewhere else on my own. It really appealed to me, I'd get away from everyone. So much for your idea that I'm the dependent type who needs to come home to a meal and a bed. No, Karen, I wanted to get out.

So instead of going home, I dossed around, walking round in my circles again. Wow, I got dizzy walking in my circles. They were unrealistic dreams, almost like wishing you could go to a desert island and live off coconuts and fish. It was my bloody unpredictability showing through, whatever that means.

Finally, I did go home. It took me to eight o'clock at night to decide. It was real dark then and I felt fragile and frost-bitten in the cold. I felt the winter that day, I only had my lightweight jacket on. I never did wear enough clothes, did I, Karen?

On top of everything else I was hungry and depressed, so I had to go somewhere, and home seemed the right place. Perhaps I'd tell Mum what was happening to me, at last I might tell her everything I'm telling you now. Then she'd understand and let me leave school and get a job.

I rehearsed all the way home what I was going to say to her. Nervously, I went over my speech as I walked up past the blue front gate and the unmown front lawn. The thought of Mum waiting for me behind the front door with gnashing teeth wasn't an exciting prospect.

My key went in the lock and the door was pushed open. I'll never forget Mum's face as I entered. It was totally broken up, with tears running down her cheeks. I remember it so well, Karen. She could hardly stop crying.

'Oh, thank God.'

'Mum.'

She was standing there like a wreck, I'd never seen her like this before. My hands touched hers by instinct.

'The school told me. All your friends said you'd finished. The school was worried and I thought you'd left us.'

'No, Mum, I was in town thinking. No need to worry.'

She was drinking a large glass of sherry. She never ever drank at home; Hell, she hardly drank, full stop.

'Edward was scared too . . .'

'I'm here, Mum.'

Still she was shaking, I tried to sit her down but she assured me that she was OK.

'You've been drinking, I thought it was a rule not to in front of Ed.'

'I broke the rule; damn it, I make them.'

I started to take my coat off and as I went to hang it up, she ran up to me and held me tight in her arms, resting her head against my body in an emotional embrace. She was crying.

'I love you, honey, I love you, I love you.'

Her face looked up at mine, 'Because I don't show it doesn't mean a thing, I find it hard. You know that.'

'Of course, Mum.'

I held her close to me; she did need me, Karen, like I needed someone. It may seem stupid to say this, but I felt like her son, bonded to her despite all her and my problems. Her love touched me. I guess it was inevitable she'd crack one day. I only wish you could have been there as well.

'I'll not leave you, Mum, I promise. On Monday I'll go back to school and it will be the same.'

What else could I say? She needed me to say it, me and Ed

were all she had and now she'd finally let go and shown how she loved me, and I felt the same for her. Having said that, I'd put myself right back in the place where I'd sworn never to go again. There was no way out, Karen. You've got to see how helplessly trapped I was. No one to help me, no one . . .

SEVENTEEN

That weekend me and Ed saw Dad for the last time before you kicked the bucket. You timed your demise so badly, what with it being a week or so before the wedding. He was all hyped up about the big day when we saw him that day at the golf club. Jill didn't come because she was making arrangements, it was like old times with the three of us. And there I am getting nostalgic again.

Ed was in form, asking the sort of questions the kid asks his grandad on those soup advertisements. It really got on my nerves.

'Daddy, why do you wear those funny hats?'

'Well, son, because it keeps out the sun.'

'Why's your ball always land a long way from the hole, Daddy?'

His unbrushed hair and open mouth looked innocently at Dad as we looked for his ball on the fairway. I looked up at the sky.

'Will you listen to the kid,' Dad laughed. 'He never stops talking. Is he like this at home?'

'Worse,' I said, cuffing him on the head. 'Except when he's playing with the Rubic cube.'

'I can do it now,' shouted out Ed, in his boastful way.

'You cheated.'

'No I didn't. I'm good.'

'Modest as well.'

'There's your ball, Dad,' I said. It was in the rough at the side of the fairway. He'd been lucky. His ball had probably hit some distant tree and bounced back onto the fairway. He played golf nearly as badly as I played pool.

'Ah yes, not a bad lie. Give me a seven iron, Jason.'

He took the club and made his customary elegant swing which was always better than the actual shot. Concentrating intensely, he fastened his gaze a hundred yards ahead where he over-optimistically hoped the ball would go. But he didn't play the shot, instead he turned to me.

'You're quiet today, Jason. In fact I've noticed it recently.'

'Am I?'

'You are, son.' He watched me as I shrugged my shoulders.

'Sorry.'

'Problems?' he probed, scratching his growing moustache. He said he was growing it for the wedding. You and Mum hated him growing a moustache, didn't you? That's probably why he was growing it; to prove he'd finally got away from Mum. 'You got problems, Jason?'

'A few.'

That's all I said. It seemed strange to talk about my life problems on a windy golf course to a guy who hardly knew me any more, not that it was his fault. Besides, he had the wedding to think about without moping over my problems.

'Is the family all right? Your mum?'

'They're fine. Karen was on the phone last night, said she was looking forward to coming to the wedding. She's got a new boyfriend.'

'It seems like a new guy each week,' he laughed. See how we talked behind your back, Karen!

Anyway he went back to his shot, trying to hit it as well as possible. Not for the first time he sliced wildly into no man's land. Kicking the grass with his heel, he muttered to himself.

'Lost ball,' screamed out Ed, so that everyone within fifty miles knew Dad had played a poor shot.

'Keep him quiet, Jason. I shouldn't really bring him along with us.'

'Yeah, he's right though, Dad. You'll not find that ball.'

Quite out of the blue he changed topic.

'I know what your problem is, Jason – girls.'

'No.'

'Hey, Jason, you've not got a girl pregnant?'

'As if I should be so lucky,' I whispered under my breath.

'Pardon?'

'I said no, I haven't put a girl up the spout.'

'Well, I don't know what your problem can be. When I was your age my problems were acne, no money and restrictive parents. You've not got the first, you have got the second and you've one restrictive parent gone except on Sundays and holidays.'

Typical Dad comment there. Real, genuine and honest, but bloody unhelpful to me. Oh Karen, his life couldn't have been so simple at sixteen. He's probably just forgotten what it was like. I bet he met a Hannah back then; I suppose we've all met at least one. I don't want to forget about mine, Karen. I want the memory of her to stick with me, always.

I got Dad to drop me off at Mr Miller's place on the way home. I'd not popped in to see him for two or three weeks, I felt guilty. Perhaps he'd cheer me up, I thought.

Quite the opposite; his life was a mess. It seemed quite a few people I knew had their lives in knots. Wow, Karen, he was a sad person. His legs and arthritis had gotten so bad that he couldn't move without pain. The result was a flat which looked even worse than my room. He hadn't bothered to do his washing up, so his kitchen was a doss-hole of mucky plates and utensils. It ponged of stale fish. The rest of the house was as bad, bookcases dusty with woodworm, unmade beds, ornaments and antiques littered at random all over the place.

'You need some home help, Mr Miller,' I said helpfully as I made him a cuppa in the kitchen. Well, I thought it was helpful.

'I most certainly do not, youngster. It's the first stage to a Home. Mrs Landell downstairs is going to a Home in Aldershot, you know, next month. Being put in by her daughter. The only advantage of me having no one is that I can't be put in a Home by anyone.'

Let me tell you, Karen, I didn't need him complaining all the time. I wasn't feeling sympathetic in the slightest.

'You're being silly, Mr Miller. Now I've brought you a cup of tea.'

'I hope it's sugared.'

'No, I put salt in today; of course it's sugared.'

He didn't thank me for the tea, snatched it out of my hands and blew it cool.

'Put the television on, youngster. There's a good film on tonight. A real film with morals.'

'Well, I don't want to miss a film with morals.'

'I'll tell you one thing, youngster. I'm ready for my time. I'm three score, ten and six in January, so I've lasted well.'

Hey, Karen, maybe you could tell me what three score, ten and six adds up to. I reckon that it's either three hundred and sixteen or seventy-six. Well, honestly, sometimes he acted as if he was three hundred and sixteen.

'Mr Miller,' I said sternly, 'this depression bit is bugging me. You seem as determined to put yourself down as you do to put down all those around you. I'm off now, and when I come to see you next I want improvements.'

Pretty un-Jay-like, huh? But I reckon you'd have done the same. It's all very well pampering people, but that's pointless if they try to drown in their own tears. My only regret was that I missed the film with morals.

It was sad that I wasn't even able to talk to Mr Miller. Alone again, Karen. Actually, coming out of old Mr Miller's house, I met Justin. He was on his bike, making as much noise as he could to impress everyone. He slowed up as he saw me walk out of the drive.

'Ah, Jay,' he heralded me. 'If it isn't the school-leaver himself. What a performance you gave on Friday.'

'Ah, it was just one of those days. I'm coming back on Monday if they'll have me back.'

'Ah, I knew you'd be back. You missed us all too much, right?'

I smiled wearily and said nothing.

'I see you've been visiting old man Miller, the grumpiest sod on the block.'

'Ah, I only popped in to check he was OK.'

That's fair enough isn't it, Karen? I wasn't aware that this was too serious a crime. Justin thought it was sensational.

'Ha, community worker now, Jay. Very nice. It makes a good story to tell the boys.'

No, Karen, I didn't argue it out. I hadn't the energy. 'Hey, Justin; get lost.'

He laughed to himself, spat out his gum and sped off. That was about the last I've spoken to Justin. All those years we'd grown up together and now I didn't care if I never spoke to him again. No, I didn't cry over it either, Karen.

EIGHTEEN

Well, Karen, that's it. Jay Border has revealed all, so to speak. I hope I didn't bore you too much, but I really did have to bore someone. Perhaps someday I'll tell all this to Edward. It could be a brother to brother talk when he's about sixteen. He could be warned about all the pot holes of being a teenager, then maybe he wouldn't fall in, like we did.

You know, Karen, I am back at Cartland, to stay. I guess I will be following in your footsteps after all. It's ironic in a way, because they nearly didn't let me in. What with all my lousy work-rate and then storming out, they thought I'd be better somewhere else, like another college. I tended to agree, but Mum begged them to let me back, so they couldn't refuse.

It's all routine once more. Cookie's back at school and predictably so are the taunts. As yet he's not walked under any buses, but nothing will surprise me now. Justin's got a 250 c.c. bike and Carl's asking out a girl in his P.E. class to a disco next week. He reckons she marks a 7.5 on the Richter Scale.

And Hannah, what about her? Well, I saw her the other day in town, quite by chance. She was in the street wearing that fabulous coat and with the same glowing eyes and soft face. I smiled at her pleasantly, but I didn't get one back, simply an acknowledgement that I was there. I still love her, Karen, I can't forget her. And yes, I still think she bursts through the Richter Scale.

Hey, I've been talking for too long. It's nippy out here and

I've still got to finish off my three miles jogging. Then I'll have completed my routine for the day.

It's been so nice talking to you, Karen. I have these visions of you looking down on me from your luxury up above. Well, I figured it would be Heaven and not Hell, even taking into account your living in sin with that Richard guy. You put in a good word for me now, for when I come up. If I'm lucky it won't be all that long. I'm dreaming again . . . wow, is it cold out here.

Also in Puffin Plus

A FOREIGN AFFAIR
John Rowe Townsend

It doesn't seem like a promising party, but when the best-looking boy in the room seeks her out, Kate is flattered. But it comes as a blow when Rudi appears equally interested in her father, a political journalist. On hearing rumours of an impending revolution in Essenheim, Kate begins to understand Rudi's dual motive, but little dreams that she too has a vital part to play in the future of that country. A funny and fast-paced story about affairs of state and affairs of the heart!

SWEET FRANNIE
Susan Sallis

Confined to a wheelchair, Fran doesn't seem to have much of a future when she goes into Thornton Hall Residential Home. But pretty soon there is eighteen-year-old Luke Hawkins to think about. After all, who better than fiercely independent Fran to help a young man who has just lost both his legs in a road accident?

DEAR SHRINK
Helen Cresswell

Oliver, William and Lucy Saxon had not been too keen on the idea of staying behind while their parents went off on a botany trip to the Amazon jungle. Had they known what the next few months had in store, they would have been horror-struck. For their relatively sheltered and happy life is swept away as disaster follows disaster.

THE VILLAGE BY THE SEA
Anita Desai

Hari and his sister, Lila, are the eldest children of an Indian family. Their mother is ill and their father spends most of his time in a drunken stupor. Grimly, Lila and Hari struggle to hold the family together until one day, in a last-ditch attempt to break out of this poverty, Hari leaves his sisters in the silent, shadowy hut and runs off to Bombay. How he and Lila cope with the harsh realities of life in city and village is vividly described in this moving and powerful story.